What Did I Do Wrong?

What Can I Do Now?

What Did I Do Wrong?

What Can I Do Now?

William & Candace
BACKUS

BETHANY HOUSE PUBLISHERS
MINNEAPOLIS, MINNESOTA 55438

Published by Bethany House Publishers
A Ministry of Bethany Fellowship, Inc.
6820 Auto Club Road, Minneapolis, Minnesota 55438

Printed in the United States of America

Library of Congress Cataloging-in-Publication Data

Backus, William D.
    What did I do wrong? What can I do now? / by William and Candace Backus.
       p. cm.

    1. Parents—Religious Life. 2. Parenting—Religious aspects—Christianity. I. Backus, Candace. II. Title.
BV4529.B28   1990
248.8'45—dc20   90-41961
ISBN 1–55661–154–4   CIP

To the memories of
our grandmothers,
Nana and Nan,
and to "the little one"

Books by Dr. Backus

Finding the Freedom of Self-Control
Finding the Freedom of Self-Control Study Guide
    (with Steven Wiese)
The Hidden Rift With God
The Paranoid Prophet
Telling Each Other the Truth
Telling the Truth to Troubled People
Telling Yourself the Truth (with Marie Chapian)
Telling Yourself the Truth Study Guide
    (with Marie Chapian)
Untwisting Twisted Relationships
    (with Candace Backus)
Untwisting Twisted Relationships Study Guide
    (with Candace Backus)
What Did I Do Wrong? What Can I Do Now?
    (with Candace Backus)
Why Do I Do What I Don't Want to Do?
    (with Marie Chapian)

Tapes by Dr. Backus

Taking Charge of Your Emotions
Telling Each Other the Truth
Telling Yourself the Truth

WILLIAM and CANDACE BACKUS live in Forest Lake, Minnesota. They serve as counselors at the Center for Christian Psychological Services, St. Paul. Candace is Vice President of Minnesota Psychtests, Inc. William is a clinical psychologist and assistant pastor of a large Lutheran church.

Contents

Introduction

"... to those who love me. ..." (Deuteronomy 5:10)

Did you endure the birth pains silently, gritting your teeth? Or did you groan and yell louder than ever in your life? No doubt you asked yourself and your obstetrician, "How much more of this can I take? Please, Doctor, give me something for the *pain!*"

All you got from the physician was "Push!"

You saw your husband standing there, looking puzzled. You wanted to cry out, "Give me some help!"

And you, Dad, how did you handle it? Did you pass endless hours the old-fashioned way, waiting in a corridor, painting mental pictures of everything that could possibly go wrong, suffering your own agony? Or were you right at her side, tears streaming down your unshaven face, sharing her pain deep within your own heart as you watched her struggle to give birth? Maybe you thought, *There's a good reason why fathers used to be confined to the waiting room!*

And then—the moment of birth! Contentment washed over you both as your little one appeared. Pain? It was worth every push and contraction! You can hardly remember it for the joy. You take turns stroking the satiny curls and the delicate skin, already hoping and dreaming the best for this "gift" now amazingly entrusted to you. . . .

When did everything begin to change? Where is that little one today? How could this teenage creature—blasting you out of the house, drumming the rock 'n roll beat with his whole body, dangling feathers from his ear, heavy chains looped around his neck, gulping milk out of the carton as it dribbles onto his dirty T-shirt, with vacant corpse-like eyes—how could he belong to you? How could this throwback to subhumanity be your little boy?

Or how could this be your darling little baby girl—the child who once won the "Integrity Award" at school, the one voted "Most Likely to Succeed"—how could this half-girl/half-woman who is living with her boyfriend in unconcerned fornication be your own flesh?

What did you do wrong?

If you are tormenting yourself with such questions, you are not alone! Many share the same heartaches. And most parents today question themselves, haunted by self-doubt, seeking some answer for distress and confusion over the behavior of grown children. And the essence of parental self-doubt is almost always the same: the feeling that you are somehow to blame for your children's problems.

Has your child, now grown up, practically severed his relationship with you? Does her hostility bubble to the surface during almost every one of her infrequent phone calls? Has your child somehow failed to mature—so that he never quite takes responsibility for his own support? Is alcohol her mainstay? Are you watching, helpless, mortified, as your child builds a criminal record, abuses drugs, gives in to sexual perversions, or becomes zombie-like with fanatic loyalty to a religious cult? Do you weep over his messy divorce, her involvement in every way-out cause from animal liberation to special privileges for gays, his repeated confinements in mental hospitals, her multiple abortions? Is there some other dysfunction or sin that has a grip on one of your children, which grieves you day and night?

Perhaps you so strenuously disapprove of what one of

your children is doing that you feel sick when you think of it. You are tormented by the thought that you have to do *something*. It's your responsibility to help—but no matter how hard you try, you can't think of a way. You feel more helpless than you've ever felt in your life.

You tell yourself: I've always wanted a close family, and a warm relationship with my children. I've prayed that they would grow up to love and respect others—their country, church, and Lord.

If you are one of the myriad of Christian parents who have prayed and worked unceasingly for your children's highest good, only to find yourself in a situation that appears nearly hopeless, we want to encourage and help you. We want to open your eyes to a new perspective in parenting older teenage and adult children. We believe you can find this perspective as you explore the Word of God, your own life, and the life of your child. Together we'll help you face some common dilemmas that confront Christian parents, check some theories about the reasons for your child's disturbing behavior. We'll explore what your responsibilities for the actions of troubled older offspring are—and which responsibilities are theirs alone.

What we offer is a twofold approach: You can allow the practical psychology of applied Christianity to unleash its changing power as you find a new honesty and freedom; and we encourage you to rely on the supernatural promises of God found in Deuteronomy 5 and Jeremiah 31: "I will show love and mercy to a thousand generations who love me and keep my commandments."

The stories we share are all true, though some are a blend of details from several family histories. Some of them are personal, some are about our friends, and some are about our clients. All—except Candy's own experiences—have been disguised for the sake of confidentiality. The people whose lives are laid bare before you are decent, honest, caring people who have questioned themselves endlessly, asking, "What were our mistakes and failures? Are we guilty? Is there hope for our child?" Our great hope for you is that strife, anguish and hopelessness will soon be re-placed by peace and great satisfaction in a renewed rela-tionship between you and your older child.

Candy and Bill Backus
Forest Lake, Minnesota
Pentecost, 1990

1

The Downward Spiral

Geraldine is a single mother whose husband, long ago, left her alone to care for their daughter. Geraldine poured her life into Kate. Now, at seventeen, Kate is close to destroying her. She comes and goes as she chooses, stays away from home for days at a time, abuses alcohol and drugs, spends nights with an ever-changing array of men, demands money and physically assaults her mother. What did Geraldine do wrong? What can she do now?

Before you read between the lines and conclude that Kate is, after all, "the product of a broken home"—consider the Swensons and the Browns.

A distinguished-looking fiftyish couple, the Swensons are heartbroken over their twenty-seven-year-old, unmarried son. Alan has turned his back on their conservative Christian tradition and joined a peculiar religious cult. They fear for his soul.

The Browns are a godly couple who devoted their lives to the Lord. Now, in their sixties, they watch in horror as their forty-year-old son pushes away from his wife and children and everything he once stood for to pursue a sinful "alternate lifestyle."

Perhaps you feel that your child is on a downward spiral, throwing away his life. It may be substance abuse, promiscuity, abuse of a spouse, a crisis pregnancy, abortion, or trouble with the law. Perhaps the child you would give your life for has lost contact with reality and lives in an unreachable world of dreams. Maybe there are sexual habits you are embarrassed even to think about. Or possibly he only talks to you with a tone of ugly resentment—and you can't think why.

And not only is he on a downward spiral, you may feel that you are on one, too. For so long you've hoped for your child to change—you've seen glimmers of change, periods of relative peace. Then the pattern of bad or destructive behavior returns. Your hopes are dashed once again. You've prayed, "Why, Lord? Why aren't you getting through to him?" With each incident you have less hope.

There is only one way to face the heartbreak of a child who is on the wrong path. That is with the assurance of God's absolute commitment to you and your child. If you are His by faith in Jesus Christ, nothing else is more powerful than this bedrock certainty. It colors everything else; it gives eternal meaning and hope for even the worst situations. Even if you haven't seen answers to your prayers for your child, even if you have given up praying, we want you to plant your feet firmly on this: God has not given up on you or that child you so deeply love.

God, too, has children. The poetic prophet Hosea expresses the pain in God's tender heart over the self-destructive behavior of His offspring, Israel:

> It was I who taught [you] to walk, taking [you] by the arms. I led them with cords of human kindness, with ties of love . . . [but] my people are determined to turn from me. How can I give you up?

Do not think for a minute that God doesn't know your pain!

We've Done Our Best

In our counseling practice, we have encountered a host of sensitive, caring Christian parents who know the same despair you feel—people who have come in tears, longing to know what they did wrong. And what they can do now.

There are the Langleys, whose promising young son recently developed a chronic mental disease from which, doctors told them, he cannot be cured.

We think of the Christensons and their frustrated desire to somehow spare their daughter, who has been convicted of grand larceny, from the hardships she will face in state prison. They ask themselves endlessly, "Couldn't we have stopped her somehow?"

Agnes's story makes us ache: Her only daughter has angrily ordered this widowed mother to stay out of her life!

We have seen hundreds of parents who have been where you are now. We've seen them weep with frustration, grieving over what they perceived as the loss of their children. We've seen hearts pierced like the heart of Mary, the Mother of Jesus, with the same sword's pointed blade.

All these parents, like you, desperately want their children to be happy, successful, healthy, productive—free from pain. God understands that desire. He placed within you a love for your child that is naturally protective and quite fierce. It is actually a form of His love within you that makes you want nothing more than to have a good relationship with your child.

Difficult as it may be to believe, a good relationship is exactly what your child also wants. Researchers Merton and Irene Strommen have demonstrated that the number one desire of children is to get along with their parents— to relate well, to understand and be understood.[1] In all probability your child, too, wants a relationship with you that is strong, loving and supportive.

If you are like most parents we counsel, it is a fair assumption that you *have* done your best, despite the human flaws we all share. And it's also a fair assumption that you've concluded your parenting skills must have been de-

---

[1]Merton P. Strommen and Irene A. Strommen, *Five Cries of Parents* (San Francisco: Harper and Row, 1985). The Strommens, well known for their research on Christian families, conducted an adolescent/parent study involving more than 8,000 adolescents and their parents.

fective. "If I hadn't made some awful mistake long ago," you tell yourself, "I wouldn't have such a problem with my kid now."

Though parents with troubled or problematic older children have one thing in common—*pain*—their situations are not all the same. For the purposes of our discussion, it will be necessary to think of three groups. For one group, the complications that beset their offspring are *chronic*, and dealing with chronic conditions requires long-term adjustments and strategies. Other parents find themselves plunged into a *crisis*, or into repeated crises, by the behavior of one or more of their children. The misfortunes of a third group cluster are their children's troubles with the law— *criminal* behavior. Let's look at each of these in turn.

The Chronic Problem

For some parents the difficulties are chronic and enduring. They may have to do with behavior—or even an emotional illness. Like the Langleys, for instance.

For Andy Langley to call us in obvious distress was, in itself, a remarkable event. One Saturday morning, Andy phoned us at home. He and his wife, Paula, wanted to talk. It sounded as if it couldn't wait.

We'd never seen this dear couple so emotional! As long as we'd known them they lived up to their Scandinavian heritage: stoic, reserved, controlled, impassive. They were also solid people of faith, whose Christianity, like their feelings, was quiet, soaked into the deeper layers of their personalities, sincere and authentic. Early in their marriage, they'd devoted themselves to intercession for their children, parents, friends, church and nation. You could count on them to plead your case, unceasingly, emphatically, before the Lord. Now they seemed nearly undone.

"We don't know how to handle what's happened," Paula began when we'd settled down in their kitchen.

"We've always been a little concerned about Luke," said Andy. "He was a loner in school. He stayed up all night sometimes, then wouldn't get up and get going in the morning. And sometimes he seemed lost in his daydreams."

"I remember you sharing some worries about Luke," Candy replied, "but you always thought he'd grow out of it."

"That's what our doctor seemed to think—for a while," Andy replied. "But the other day we took Luke in for a physical. He seemed so listless and unmotivated, Paula thought he might be sick. The doctor referred us to a psychiatrist." Andy's eyes filled with tears. "The psychiatrist said Luke has *schizophrenia.*"

"We don't know what to do," Paula interjected, her eyes welling also. "We're so upset. Seems as if he's never going to be normal—almost like our Luke is dead." At that, tears brimmed over onto her cheeks.

We could offer them comfort—but no "quick answers." We've watched as their faith, which once appeared so rock-like, has been sorely tried. They've stood by, helpless, while Luke flounders from job to job, remains aloof and withdrawn at family gatherings, sits around watching television and muttering to himself. Reluctantly, they've given up their dream of a college education for their son, a career and a home, grandchildren.

Today the Langleys are left with more questions than answers. "Did we do something to Luke long ago to cause this illness?" they ask. "Is his misery our fault? What can we do to help him? Are we being manipulative if we let him know we expect him to take some responsibilities? Will we make him worse if we treat him like anyone else? Should we nag him to take his medications? He hates them! What if we push him over the edge?"

The Langleys' problem is, of course, only one type of chronic difficulty for which a parent may feel responsible. Other chronic problems may have molded the pattern of your child's life for a few months, for several years—perhaps for a lifetime. We hurt for our children whenever they have a chronic problem, even if it's only smelly feet. For you the unrelenting fallout continues to take its toll. Among the many problems that can beset parents, certain emotional and behavioral problems cause more intense anguish than others.

Rebellion

You have locked horns with this child since he or she was eight. Now the "sweet little girl" has become a tramp-like woman, sneaking out of the house at night, staying God knows where until all hours. The little boy who was the delight of the Sunday school has, at seventeen, begun to pull away from the Christian morality you so carefully taught him. Not only has be begun to hide *Penthouse* under his pillow, but he's written articles for the school paper, criticizing "fundamentalist" morality. You can see the slow, simmering rebellion in his eyes.

Depression

Perhaps your child has, for months or years, exhibited recurring periods of sadness, lethargy and negative or pessimistic attitudes about life. Hopeless about the future, down on himself, uninterested in daily life, he worries you sick by revealing thoughts of suicide. All the reassurance you've given hasn't helped him feel any less worthless. You are at your wits' end, discouraged and down on yourself.

Schizophrenia

If your child, like Luke, carries this diagnosis, he was always the one who didn't fit in, the youngster who was teased and persecuted for a certain strangeness. You wondered why no one wanted to reach out to him, why teachers took so little interest, why he had so few friends and rarely got invited to play with other kids. You couldn't grasp why his achievements were usually marginal, his grades spotty, his attempts to learn a skill so unsuccessful. And why did he seem to live in a world of his own? You heard him up at night when the rest of the household slept; you wondered why, and what he was doing. Possibly he sat for hours, rocking or staring into space or listening to inner voices. As time went on, he would quit good jobs without warning or withdraw from college just when things seemed to you to be going better. Later, perhaps, you were told point blank that your precious child was schizophrenic, saddled with an incurable mental disease, and that he would have to be on powerful medication for the rest of his life.

How helpless you felt! How alone! Maybe you even felt deserted by God.

Severe interpersonal conflicts

Has your child never gotten along with *anybody*? Not even with you? Has he always been argumentative, constantly challenging his teachers and fighting with peers? This is the kind of child who can't hang on to friendships because his quarreling alienates everyone. Several employers have fired him. His marriage has folded. You have to watch what you say or he'll blow up at you and end the conversation, maybe even the relationship. You long to hold on—but you've got a raging tiger by the tail.

Homosexuality

Has he only hinted at his preference for male lovers—or told you defiantly that he is what he is and he's tired of hiding it just to please you? Has he diagnosed you as "homophobic"—afraid of homosexuals? Frequenting gay bars, having sex with multiple partners, the child you raised does things with his body that turn your stomach. And you're terrified—certain he'll die from AIDS.

Has she declared her "right" to live with another woman? Has she instructed you in her *avant garde* morality, implying that you ought to be ashamed of yourself for remaining so hopelessly mired in outdated, sexually repressive "prejudices"? Does your heart break when she comes home with her "friend"?

The Crisis Problem

The *crisis* usually comes as a surprise. Just when you thought things were working out for your child, he goes and pulls *this!* Because it likely involves other people, the problem may have long-term ramifications.

Roger and Teresa described their lives as "one emotional earthquake after another." Their daughter Stephanie keeps dropping bombshells, plunging them into crises with her.

A strikingly handsome, idealistic Christian couple, Roger and Teresa always wanted to help make the world a better place. Ironically, their troubles began on a day long ago when they waited at the airport gate with their blond, blue-eyed toddler, Jenny, to receive a diminutive bundle of joy from India. Stephanie, it turned out, was every bit as adorable as Jenny, with her blue-black wavy hair and huge brown eyes. Unlike Jenny, though, this child had been hurt. Although she was only three, her wariness suggested abuses and neglect they could only guess at.

All the more reason to love her, thought Roger and Teresa. They committed themselves to her care, certain that their love would bathe away every trace of Stephanie's early suffering due to the cruelty and lust of adults. *Surely,* Stephanie could be made whole by her parents' devotion. Surely.

It didn't work that way. Never once had Roger and Teresa imagined that their beloved daughter would grow up and "turn" on them, and on herself, with hatred borne of her deeply ingrained conviction that she was worthless. A single out-of-wedlock pregnancy might be a sad mistake, but when Roger and Teresa sought our help, Stephanie had informed them her *third* child was due.

"Where did we go wrong?" they pleaded. "Didn't we give her our very best? Will she ever know how much we love her? Doesn't she care? Can she possibly understand the grief we feel for her? If she doesn't care about us, shouldn't she care for herself and for her children? How can she abuse them and herself so? We don't understand."

Teresa had been crying herself to sleep each night, while Roger held his ache inside. Though they knew Jesus as a Lord who wept with them, they were convinced they had failed Him somehow. "It has to be our fault. Is this a punishment? What did we do that's made our prayers so futile?"

Many sons and daughters plunge their families into a one-time crisis. Most learn from the experience and go on, never again to cause the roof to fall in. For some of you, though, crisis is an everyday word. You can hardly remember when you didn't live in a boiling cauldron of turmoil. You tense up when things appear normal because you're sure the next crisis is about to break over your head. All along—grieving over your child, striving to keep yourself together—you put up with those interminable spells of accusing silence, or dark looks of anger (directed for unknown reasons at you), or with the child's maddening insistence that nothing is wrong. It's the world—the world is against them. Will the crises never end?

The Criminal Problem

What a shock it is to come face-to-face with this one: Your son or daughter has committed a crime—maybe more than one—and is now indelibly branded a *convict!* It may have begun with no more than a little wayward rebellion—"Just a strong-willed child," you said. "It's just experimentation. Just for the fun of it." And you may have been right.

But the System is involved: courts, judges, probation officers, halfway houses, institutions, jails. It's out of your hands—another terror. Now what happens to your child? To you? Will your life's savings be drained by attorneys, counselors, court costs? How will you ever face your friends without seeing disapproval in their eyes?

Parents whose older children are in legal trouble tend to think of their children's needs above everything else. Working with parents whose older children have been in trouble—for using or selling drugs, theft, rape, incest, deviant sexual behavior, prostitution, fraud, or abuse—we've found that few such parents ask help for themselves, though their own need is so great. More than anything on earth, they want what is good for their children. But these parents need help for themselves, too! We try to give them relief from their own anguish and an end to self-castigation. Most often they are good people who feel responsible for the actions of the *ir*responsible.

If you are one of those who has had to face your child's criminal actions—even to the point, perhaps, where you instigated an arrest because it was the only way to halt the race toward self-destruction—you know too well the struggle you wage against self-accusation and despair.

To all those parents who are suffering, we say it is time to take a fresh look at yourself. Perhaps you've poured your attention and energy into the life of your child for so long that it's been years since you stepped back and took a look at your own life. Maybe you've even forgotten how to *live* a normal life! Though your offspring's problems may persist, you can stop your own downward spiral under the weight of fear, guilt, and remorse.

Our aim is to help you address your own needs and find new strength, comfort, healing, freedom. The first step is to gain freedom from the three main inner enemies—fear, guilt, and remorse—which cripple your spirit. Beyond that, we want to help you re-open communication and foster forgiveness. Ultimately, no matter what your circumstances, we want to help you learn how to enter into the "rest" that God has promised. (See Hebrews 4.)

As counselors—and as parents!—we can assure you that what God offers is hope for better things to come. That hope was confirmed when He sent His own Son to die for you *and* your children. He is *for* you!

So it's with this unshakable hope that we can confront the first and greatest of our inner enemies. That enemy is fear.

Take a little time to be alone. Ask yourself: Do I know what my child's real, inner problems are? Do I spend time blaming myself or others for the problems of my child? Am I willing to be changed myself as part of the solution to this problem?

2

Fear

Do you remember those early days—the time you brought your first little one home to sleep in his own bassinet? You got up to check and see if he was still breathing properly. A cold hand touched your soul when you thought that little form was too still. Remember your panic when you caught him in his first lie—and you were sure he'd develop into a pathological liar? Or the fear you felt when you met her first heartthrob and knew that she was too young and naive to cope with those scheming boys! Then there were those trying late-teen years when you'd wake up at 2 A.M., and find that she wasn't in yet. You were convinced she'd been kidnapped, injured, or killed in a car crash. Chances are, you've known fears never dreamed of by those who bypass parenthood!

Most of our parental fears are needless. Yet, in the case of your older problem child, it became clear at some point that something really had gone wrong. And since then, you've been embroiled in a tangle of fearful thoughts that don't go away.

Real fears hang on, and their weight slowly draws the life out of you.

What are the signs of this chronic, embedded fear? No doubt you know some of them. You wake out of a sound sleep, with mental images that foreshadow the inevitable disaster. And not only are they playing on your mind's silver screen in the dark at three in the morning, they're still vivid in the clear light of day. You know the flash of fear when the phone rings and you hear the voice of your problem child on the other end of the line. What now? What catastrophe will this call reveal? When your friends tell you of their children's successes, your fears for your child choke off any happiness you might feel for others.

Even in moments when you could be relaxing, all the conceivable unhappy outcomes for your child present themselves to your imagination. What's going to happen to him? He's withdrawing more and more. Will he end up isolating himself, even from his family? You worry—*always*—because she does nothing except stay in her room and listen to that awful music. What can be going on inside her mind? Could she be under some sort of spiritual bondage? Where will it end?

Here are a host of fears and "what ifs" you may recognize:

He won't have any friends, ever—I just know it. She's so gullible, there's nobody to protect her, she's going to be ripped off. He's got that low-level job—what if he never gets anywhere economically, and can't even take care of himself? What if she blows her mind on those drugs, and ends up on a back ward in a state hospital? That wild crowd she hangs out with—what if she marries somebody who abuses her? What if he ends up in prison? What if he loses his faith altogether? What if she goes to hell?

What's going to happen to my child?

One couple with an older problem child manages to live with ever-present fear by fighting such thoughts constantly. "We try to keep busy with other things so we won't think about it. We try not to talk about it too often. It works pretty well—until something else happens to remind us. Then all the fears come back in force." Sound familiar?

Even if most of your fears and worries concern your child, it's likely that you'll have some fears for yourself, too.

You foresee having to pay damages for your child's mistakes, or for treatment or counseling. What will it cost you? Will you lose all your savings? Will you cross over the poverty line?

You worry about embarrassment. How will you be able to look your friends in the eye? How can you face the other people at your church? What will your relatives say about you for having such a problem child? Maybe you'll want to avoid everybody when it all comes out.

And what about the inner pain? How much grief and anguish will you be able to stand? What if something happens that is so awful you can't handle it? Will you crack up? Will you lose your faith in God? Will you make yourself sick with worry?

And what about your spiritual strength—your faith? What if you become cynical because nothing helps and God doesn't seem to hear your prayers? What if you lose your faith, become hard and untrusting? Like one father who—contemplating his daughter's fourth pregnancy out of wedlock—turned bitter and resentful. "I think I'll just tell her to get an abortion!" he muttered. And this, even though he's taken a strong stand against abortion, believing it to be murder. The words were his way of expressing worry and hopelessness. Are you afraid you yourself might end up compromising your own moral convictions, driven there by overpowering fear?

The truth about fear, however, is that it need not be overpowering. The first step in defeating the looming monster of fear is really very simple—yet it seems difficult for many Christians.

Unfortunately, much Christian teaching seems to give the impression that a truly faithful Christian will never experience fear or any other negative emotion. Perhaps you've been told point-blank that you're wrong for having any fears, or that the fact that you experience fear must indicate what a weak Christian you are. This is absolutely untrue. It is normal to have fear.

What we want you to know is that you don't have to let fear control you. You don't have to be victimized and totalled-out by your fears. Even when there appears to be nothing you can do about your child's problem beyond praying for him, you don't have to meekly resign yourself to a lifetime of fretful worry.

Later on, we'll show you how to apply some powerful truths, based on God's promises, to help you get a handle on negative, life-draining emotions. For now, it's important to take a look at fear's varying effects on different people.

The Wedge of Fear

Josh seemed to be on his way to health and wholeness. He'd even been leading a support group for addictive adults.

Then one night, he and some old friends from his past went out driving. He didn't really mean for it to happen, but it did. Josh started drinking again, telling himself that he would sober up tomorrow. He'd *really* quit tomorrow—this time for sure. But for now, he'd just enjoy himself. . . .

Later, he saw the flashing red lights in his rearview mirror, coming closer and closer. He tried to outrun the police. When they finally stopped him, he fought and kicked until the officers had no recourse but to restrain him. Josh was drunk and in trouble. Again.

After getting her son's phone call from jail, Josh's mother, Carol, anguished over him. She wondered if this would be the time he'd finally be sent to the workhouse. She hoped it would be, all the while hurting for her son. Carol could see that if Josh continued on the path he'd been on for twenty-seven years, he would soon kill himself, or worse, kill some innocent person with his reckless, drunk driving. She began to pray that things would not go easily for him.

Mark, Josh's father, felt differently. He went to the jail to bail his son out. Then he proceeded to the place where Josh's car had been taken, to bail it out so his son would be able to drive to work the next day. Mark felt that he was doing the right thing for Josh. Mark feared for his son, that he wouldn't be able to keep up with his work and support his family. To Mark, the worst possible thing was to see Josh go to jail.

What we can glean from these parents is how differently we each respond to fear for our children. Mark wanted to remove the immediate pain from his son; Carol wanted to remove the possibility of worse pain down the road. Mark was seeking to solve Josh's problems for him; Carol was willing to put her son in the hands of God, for Him to deal a severe mercy toward Josh. Mark thought he was doing the Christian thing—showing forgiveness and acceptance for Josh—and he thought his wife was cold and hard because she didn't agree. Carol thought her husband was a sucker and was helping to send their son to an early death by continuing to bail him out.

As you can no doubt see, fear has a way of working its hooks into a parent's soul. Suddenly, you feel you're no longer in control; larger forces are sweeping you toward dangerous ends.

Once you understand what fear itself is doing to you, you can begin to overcome. The following are some of fear's effects to watch out for:

Fear paralyzes

Steve has lived a life of dishonesty for twenty-three years. Now that he has finally been caught taking bribes and gambling, his future looks bleak. His reputation has been ruined, and his wife of three years is leaving him, taking their one-year-old daughter with her. Steve returns to his one hope for help: Mom and Dad.

His parents struggle over what to do for Steve. Should they allow themselves to get involved again? Or should they concentrate their efforts on prayer? Should they boot him out of the house before he has a chance to ruin them, as he ruined himself, his wife and their child? Steve's parents feel so emotionally traumatized that they have difficulty thinking clearly. The problem looms over them, appearing so big and impossible their hope fades.

Because they are overwhelmed by the whole picture,

these parents need to take just one small step. They should turn to one person—a pastor, a counselor or a trusted friend—who can help guide them toward objectivity and direction. This person may not be an "expert" in dealing with family difficulties, but even a listening ear and heart will help these parents sort out their own emotions from fact and reality. This first step is the starting point; the rest will unfold in time.

Fear divides

The story of Josh and his parents is common to many families. The parents argue over what each thinks is best for their child. "If only you had done this . . . ," "If only you had been a better parent, this never would have happened. . . ." These bitter phrases often replace focusing on the real problem. The parents are pitted against each other and the important objective is forgotten. The fear of what is happening to them and their child overrides the ability to see the problem, and therefore a possible solution, clearly.

These parents must not allow their emotions, false guilt and blame to divide them from each other. They, of all people, are wise to the ways of their child. With an awareness that the devil is at work to destroy, parents can unite as one force to overcome their own fears and march together to do battle for their child.

Fear steals energy

Josh's dad was so fearful of what would happen if Josh went to jail that he did whatever he could to avoid this consequence of his son's behavior. He put up money for bail and attempted to convince the authorities that all Josh needed was another chance. This father failed to see that such efforts only confirmed Josh's irresponsibility. In the long run, Josh is merely biding his time until he can get drunk and violent again with his old buddies.

Much valuable time and opportunity are wasted when

people deal only with the symptoms, ignoring the problem itself. Then when the parent is finally ready to concentrate on the real issue, he finds himself exhausted. Time, resources, and energy have been frittered away applying Band-Aids to wounds that require stitches!

Parents can become strong and full of courage in heart, soul and mind by drawing strength from Jesus Christ, the promises of God's Word, and godly friends and counselors. Then they will be able to help their child in the way that is best for the whole family.

"Fear Not. . . ."

In the Gospel of Luke, Jesus reminds us that the number of hairs on your head are known to God. God cares greatly, even for the little birds of the air. He provides for them abundantly. The lilies that do nothing to earn their keep are clothed in glory and magnificence.

Jesus tells us over and over not to worry or fear, but to seek His kingdom, and everything else will be added to us, because He loves us. Where our treasure is, He says, there will our heart be also. (See Luke 12.)

May we be found treasuring the Lord, listening intently to His Word, replacing fear with the knowledge of His constant love and concern for us and for our beloved children.

List your three greatest fears for your problem child. See Isaiah 43:1–7, and let the Word of God speak to you.

3

Guilt

Unfortunately, becoming a parent in the twentieth century often means buying a $250,000 ticket for the guilt trip of your life. Having read Freud and Spock in graduate school, a great army of "professionals" have worked to correct the assumed ignorance of young parents—passing on the conclusion that we parents are primarily responsible for "warping" our children. As a result, several generations of mothers and fathers believe that whatever we do, it's usually *wrong!*

No matter that so many of these "professionals" have had little or no experience in actual child-rearing! No matter that the experts rampantly contradict one another. It's become axiomatic: parenting is laced with uncertainty and guilt. Most of us forget there was a time, several generations ago, when young parents thought they knew what they were doing merely because they emulated their own parents. Today, on the contrary, we consider our own parents' method of child-rearing a benchmark to move *away* from. ("I'm not going to make *my* kids sit and practice piano by the hour! What good did it do me?") We devour books with titles like *How to Spank and When, When Children Misbehave, What to Do If Your Child Is a Pain, Making a Family Happy, Being a Christian Parent,*

Ten Tips for Parents, Handling the Aggressive Child, and more—tons more. But few books have been offered on dealing with the *guilt,* the sense of inadequacy haunting nearly every one of us—especially those whose children have not turned out quite as well as the books and experts suggested they should.

For many parents, vague feelings of guilt are a familiar companion. Since you first looked into your newborn infant's face, a shadow of self-doubt has lurked in a corner of your mind, just waiting for that kid to develop a problem! When a difficulty comes it triggers an explosion of guilty feelings. And much more so if your child has come to adulthood with major problems.

Coping with your situation requires that you resolve in a healthy way your own struggles with *guilt, guilt feelings,* and a sense of *shame.* These are three related burdens, and it's important that we differentiate between them.

Guilt

Guilt may or may not be accompanied by guilty feelings. You can be guilty without any awareness of the truth. Guilt describes the state of a person who has broken the law of man or of God.

Let's say, for example, that you honestly did not see the stop sign, so you drove through an intersection without even slowing down. Blissfully unaware of your status as a lawbreaker, you puzzle over those flashing red lights in your rearview mirror. Quickly, it dawns on you that those lights are attached to a squad car. You pull over, and you discover what you did wrong. As soon as the officer drives away, you drive back to the intersection and, sure enough, there is the big red octagonal sign. How on earth did you miss it?

Here's the question: Are you innocent? You don't *feel* guilty. But does the absence of guilt feelings mean you are innocent? *No.* Guilt is an objective state of affairs, the predicament you are in after breaking a law. So you *can* be guilty without having guilt feelings.

In a similar way, you can be guilty of breaking God's law—of sinning—without awareness of wrongdoing or feelings of guilt. As this relates to your child, you may be able to say honestly, "I didn't realize how angry I was, or how unfairly I was treating Johnny!" But this does not excuse you from having treated him unfairly.

A second aspect of guilt is that it is universal. Not one of us can truthfully declare ourselves guiltless. As Paul says, "I know that nothing good lives in me, that is, in my sinful nature" (Romans 7:18). And, "The sinful nature desires what is contrary to the Spirit, and the Spirit what is contrary to the sinful nature. They are in conflict with each other, so that you do not do what you want" (Galatians 5:17).

On a day-to-day level, most of us spend a lot of energy trying to deflect accusations, especially accusations from our children. Of course, there are times when we're *not* guilty exactly as charged. But it's also true that every one of us has pride at work within—a pride that hates and refuses correction and constructive criticism, especially when a flaw or mistake is pointed out by our own children! If we are honest, though, not one of us can look our child in the eye and say, "I've never sinned against you." Whether we *feel* bad or not, there were times when we did wrong in our role as parents. In a moment, we'll face some common parental sins.

Sorting Through the Haze of Guilt

How do guilt feelings fit into the picture? The fact is, feelings may or may not be "correct"—that is, they may or may not point to real guilt. Therefore, guilt feelings are unreliable.

Guilt feelings were meant to perform an important function: calling our attention to behavior that is morally and spiritually wrong. Because most of us have a conscience, we feel bad if we think we've done something sinful. It is the God-ordained job of conscience to get our attention and even to punish us when we do wrong. To that end, conscience properly afflicts us with painful guilty feelings. Though it's hard to describe the sensation exactly, when you feel guilty, you feel like hiding, staying out of the light, not looking anyone in the eye, and as if you are about to be stricken with a terrible punishment. God's purpose for instilling in us the capacity to feel guilt is to motivate us to make amends to the person we've injured and to God.

Of course the question we're facing is this: Is your guilt over your child's behavior *real*—that is, based on a sin you committed—or is it a feeling only? It is very important, as you work toward inner freedom, that you allow the Holy Spirit to help you sort out fact from feeling. This is the only way you can find solid footing again, and escape from the downward spiral. Painful as it may be, real sins must be faced.

What sins *did* you commit against your child? Were you inconsistent—too strict at times, too lenient at others, too vacillating, too unstable? Did you sin against God and your family by being a super-Christian one day, then turning your back on God when things went wrong? Were you abusive, ungracious, unkind, overbearing, ill-mannered? Did you use your child as a sex object? Did you knowingly risk his life and health, exposing your child to needless hazard? Did you let someone else abuse your child while you stood by, afraid to intervene? Did you destroy your child's spirit, attacking him verbally?

Is it possible that your relationship with your child is impaired at this moment because you won't bend, won't forgive, won't tell your child the truth, won't admit wrongdoing? Is it possible that your child is having difficulties with you today because past sins against him have not been dealt with?

Some sins are the "garden variety" type, not that they are "less" in God's sight, but they can be attributed to any one of us. For instance, you lost your temper sometimes. You put your child down for mistakes instead of praising him for what he did right. You put off spending time with your daughter when she needed you. You were the kind who would rather do it yourself than teach your son. You criticized or nagged. Maybe you can remember feeling a constant anger at your children; possibly you felt disappointment in them; you compared them unfavorably with someone else's children, and wanted to get away from them. If you have never faced up to sins like these, you must take that all-important step—for your own sake *and* the sake of your child.

We will discuss recovery from real guilt in a moment. But first, it's important to examine inappropriate feelings of guilt and shame.

Guilt *Feelings*

Much that parents feel guilty about is not sin. Let's say you took a job that paid well but kept you away from home too much. You tried to compensate by setting clear guidelines and a good example—but with hindsight you now see clearly that more direct contact with your child might have changed things. As a result, you feel stained with guilt over good things you *didn't* do, or didn't do *enough* of.

We have this to say about the "not enough": If you want to torment yourself with guilt for any reason, just start contemplating all the "not enoughs" of which you can accuse yourself! Maybe you didn't offer your child enough "opportunities" like music lessons. Or you didn't talk to your child about his feelings enough. Or you didn't invite his friends over often enough. Or you weren't dedicated enough to your child. Read the following list and see how quickly guilt feelings begin to stir:

    not committed enough
    not attentive enough
    not helpful enough with schoolwork
    not loving enough
    not enough time spent
    not enough praise

not enough discipline
not enough understanding
not enough money
not enough firmness
not enough consistency
not enough freedom
not enough control
not enough encouragement
not enough explanation of the reasons for your rules

The truth is, of some things there is *never* enough. Who couldn't stand more love, more praise, more help, more consideration? Who among us wouldn't gladly be more caring, more faithful, more trusting, more selfless, more wise, more skilled? Unfortunately, many of us pick up guilt feelings from reading well-intended books on parenting—many of which seem to offer "the keys" to wiser, better parenting that will be "enough." When will we come to understand the truth that—excuses and sins notwithstanding—only God's parenting is enough? Our parenting is only a shadow of His.

Our point here is to say, don't become a victim of a "not enough" list. Deal with real guilt that is gently revealed by the Holy Spirit—not with the condemning voice of deadly self-criticism.

Shame

Many of us confuse guilt and *shame*, though there is a vast difference between the two. Guilt, as we've said, pertains to transgression against God and the law. Shame is related to our need for the approval of other people. Shame has to do with our fear of human opinions, while guilt has to do with our spiritual state before God.

Currently, shame has acquired a bad name in many circles. Some "experts" say you ought never to feel shame about anything, and if you do you're sick. This is untrue. Shame does have its place as long as it is not the main, controlling impulse of your life. There is nothing wrong with caring what others think, or with making reasonable efforts to keep their good opinion of you. Nor is it bad to try to please those whose judgment matters to you. "Be careful to do what is right in the eyes of everybody," Paul wrote. "If it is possible, as far as it depends on you, live at peace with everyone" (Romans 12:18). It is our opinion that, just as guilt feelings can be an appropriate warning bell, so shame can alert us to a need for changes in our parenting behavior. When we concern ourselves with the judgments of other people (shame) more intensely than we attend to the judgments of God (guilt), we are on the wrong track.

Consider some examples: Your mother-in-law says you weren't strict enough. Your neighbor points out that you were too severe because you made your child come inside at 8:00, while her kids got to play outside until 9:00. Your grown child says you are an "old-fashioned" legalist, utterly incapable of understanding where he's coming from. If you are tormented, trying hard to defend and justify, then it may be that you are a victim of shame—the dominating need for others to agree that you are right.

Shame may be the motivator when you compare your own family adversely with those impossible squeaky-cleans, the fault free family of Peter and Priscilla Perfect and their Perpetually Prim Perfectettes, Pammy, Pippy, and Peppy. (Your kids are stuck with names like Don, Jake, Steve, Margie and Bonnie! What's more, your boys' shirttails are usually out and your girls want to play football instead of cutting paper dolls.)

Release From False Guilt Feelings

Most parents afflict themselves with false guilt feelings at least some of the time. Some people, however, feel guilty all the time. Ever ready to blame themselves, they rarely feel free.

If you are a parent who nags yourself with guilty feelings when you haven't done anything wrong, it's possible that you harbor a *radical misbelief*—that is, a strongly held erroneous belief upon which you base your view of yourself and others. To further define what we mean, we offer a true-life illustration.

One young parent told Bill how he had come to invent the belief that he was utterly responsible for everything that went wrong in his household. His own father, a farmer, became angry with Marc when rain ruined some hay which had been cut but not bailed. A teenager at the time, Marc was blamed for this and several other costly accidents. At length he came to believe that he would always be held responsible even if he was innocent. He was responsible for everything! Therefore, if anything went wrong, he would be punished. He shouldered the unbearable weight of believing that he had to struggle to be perfect: *Everything*, even an accident, was his responsibility.

When Marc became a parent, he had grown to believe that he was ultimately guilty for the bad behavior of his children. It is important for you to recognize the connection—as Marc did—between his hunger for approval and the untruth he lived by: "Unless everything is perfect, I am somehow to blame."

Other radical misbeliefs a parent may hold are these:

- If I make any mistakes as a parent, I am an awful person.
- If anything is wrong in the behavior of my older offspring, I am guilty of having failed somewhere.
- I am a bad person who hasn't managed to make everything right for my family.

What happens when such thoughts are carving a deep rut through that part of your mind psychologists have called "the internal monologue"? How would such thoughts make you feel? Happy? Free? Satisfied? Fulfilled? Able to enjoy your children and grandchildren? Hardly. Such thoughts would cripple and kill the enjoyment of life. It would be nearly impossible to have any fun with your offspring because being around them would only turn up the volume of that nagging inner voice.

But suppose you're tired of carrying guilt—and we

hope that you are! Suppose you want to uncover any radical misbeliefs and get free of them. What do you do?

First, take some time to think about a situation that makes you feel guilty. Why do you feel responsible? Write out your radical misbelief so that you can see it in black and white.

For example, you might feel guilty because your son or daughter has cheated on his or her spouse. In the quiet of your mind a voice is saying, "You are somehow responsible." Be bold enough to ask, "Why?" The answer that may come back is, "You didn't instill stronger Christian values in your child." Again, a question: "Can any parent insure that a child will pick up and always live by a strong moral code?" The true answer is *no*.

Second, reexamine your misbelief—in this case it is simply: "I am a bad parent because my adult child failed to be honorable and sinned through infidelity." Do you see how silly this is? Soak up the fact that your radical misbelief is *false*, even meaningless.

The fact is, you will be confronted with this old, inaccurate line of thinking over and over before you get free of it. You must work at reminding yourself that your offspring is a responsible being, capable of making his own choices. (Goodness knows, our children have found it easy to ignore our suggestions in the past! They went out of their way to ignore us when they were adolescents, and they still do! Moreover, we are not responsible for preventing every catastrophe. That would make us God!)

Gradually, instead of the terrible feelings of false guilt, you'll find yourself enjoying contentment, freedom, peace and joy. And those emotions make a far better spiritual base for working through your tough relationship. That is the kind of solidity you need.

What to Do About Shame

If shame is a problem for you, it's likely that you are living by a faulty rule which, if spoken, might sound something like this:

"What other people think about me is so important I must make sure their thoughts about me are positive."

Spin-off misbeliefs from this root might include such wrong assumptions as these:

- If someone disapproves of me or my child, I'm a failure.
- I have to make people think my family and I are better than we are.
- If my child thinks I'm not a perfect parent, I must be a bad person.
- My child's disordered emotions and actions embarrass me because others will think I'm a bad parent.
- I can't let anybody know the awful truth about my child.

As you can see, motivation by shame can cause you to live behind a false front, constantly burdened with an impossible task—making others think well of you.

The remedy is to plant the truth firmly in your mind and spirit. Truth will set you free from the misery of living in shame. When you believe and coach yourself with the truth, you'll stop being a slave to the judgments, criticism, and opinions of other people. This will take practice.

Here is the truth, over and against the shame misbelief:

Although I do care reasonably about the reactions and opinions of people I value, I can stand it if they don't agree with me. So when I believe I'm in God's will, the verdicts of most other people matter very little or not at all.

Some other truths to tell yourself when you're battling shame:

- My child's problems do *not* mean I'm a failure, and I will stop telling myself it's the end of the world when someone else knows about our troubles or disapproves of me because of them.
- I don't have to have a guarantee that every person I know thinks that I and my family are perfect.

- People don't have to think I'm a better parent than I actually am.
- It's more important for me to be open and truthful than to fabricate a false public image.

Let yourself open up. You may want to start with one close Christian friend or counselor. That may seem threatening, but, as is true with most of our fears, the results will not be as horrible as you imagine. You may discover that most people will eagerly offer their prayers, concern and support. You may be surprised to learn that some folks you esteem very highly are suffering similar parenting difficulties. Even if some people offer you only misunderstanding and harsh reproach, their negative reactions aren't going to wipe you out. Perhaps you will eventually find it an important part of your cure to learn that you can tolerate others' disapproval—that it's even possible for God to use such unpleasantness to reveal to you areas in which you are maturing.

What to Do About Real Guilt

Earlier in this chapter, we talked about letting the Holy Spirit help you locate real guilt. The work of God's Spirit is quite remarkable. Though it may carry a sting, it's a cleansing, healthy, good feeling at the same time. Here are some examples of real guilt.

There's Glenda, a recovering alcoholic, who would give anything now to take back the abusive outbursts she once used to intimidate and emasculate her twelve-year-old son.

There's Marlin, who knew that his ten-year-old daughter was repeatedly fondled by his best friend, yet he did not protect her. Marlin hated himself for this sin against his daughter and he was truly guilty.

Maybe you too have to face some pretty grim offenses. Did you deliberately sacrifice your child's well-being rather than stand up to an abusive mate? Did you inflict emotional or physical abuse on your child? Did you deliberately deprive your child of necessities so you could have "toys"—motorcycles, expensive vacations, boats, the latest in clothes? Did you live such a bad example that you taught your child to lie, steal, cheat?

Many of us feel the pain of more common human failings—simple selfishness, anger, a critical nature, or the tendency to be overly demanding.

Whatever the case, if your guilt is real, then you need a Savior. There is only One.

Perhaps you already know Jesus Christ as your Savior. But you haven't experienced His promise to put your parenting sins away from you as far as east is from west (Psalm 103:12). Yet Christ's life and His death on the cross as your substitute satisfied God's anger at the selfish decisions you made at your child's expense. By His victory over sin, Jesus has the power to eradicate all your sins, releasing you from the load forever. He can do this because He already suffered the whole penalty for them on the cross. If you are ready to lay your sins on Jesus, to let Him take the burden of them as He desires to do, here is a way to do it:

Confess your sins. You may never have done this because you didn't know how, or because you didn't want to face them. But the Bible never urges us to just forget about our sins. Rather, it says, "if we confess our sins He is faithful and just and will forgive us our sins and purify us from all unrighteousness" (1 John 1:9). Because God's desire is to forgive and cleanse, you can pray, "Father, I have sinned against you by sinning against my child. This is what I have done. . . ." He will hear and forgive.

Remind yourself daily: "Jesus died on the cross for these sins. I am going to believe that they are now being taken away, as far as east is from west. His death is powerful enough to remove even sins as great as mine. He is cleansing me now and making me perfect and whole."

Tell yourself: "I am going to make amends to my child for having hurt him. I will try to find a way to own up to what I did and admit it to my child. And with God's grace, I am going to work on building a new relationship with my child from this moment on." In a later chapter, we will explore ways you can take this challenging step.

These three steps comprise what Scripture calls *repentance,* or getting a new mind. It is your part in finding release from sin and guilt. Repentance is what puts you on God's side, and with so powerful and reliable an ally, you can also combat the next great inner enemy—remorse.

Think of the distinctions between guilt, guilt feelings, and shame. Then from your own life give an example of each one. Meditate on Isaiah 1:18.

4

Remorse

Christians so often suffer under the impression that they must always look happy, say they are cheerful, and hide their truest feelings even from themselves under a plastic veneer of "joy!" Somehow many believe that if we *act* happy, we will *be* happy.

Chances are when your child is struggling, you are anything but happy. You worry about your child. And though you've prayed, tried to read your Bible more, and done everything you can think of to find a solution, the problem hasn't dissolved. It seems to stick closer to you than your own shadow.

Hidden beneath your fears—hidden, even beneath the vague sense of guilt you've carried—may lie another inner enemy: *remorse.*

Remorse can be more than a flicker of sadness at chances missed—it can be like a deep chasm of many sadnesses. Remorse is the open grave of images of what once *was*—memories of your child's innocence, precious moments—all that now seems lost. It's filled with depressing images of what could be right *now*, if your child's life were not in upheaval. And it's filled with haunting images of what may never be in the *future*. And the walls of this chasm are built by your own sense of failure and inadequacy. It is truly a hellish pit.

Remorse may be so deep within you that you are not even aware of its full power—though it is draining the life out of you.

Dolores came to us after months of taking medication for headaches and lower back pains to little avail. She'd been offended when her physician referred her to a psychology clinic. "I don't know why I'm here," she told Bill, smiling brightly. "My problem is headaches and awful back pain. I don't see what a psychologist can do about that!"

Bill admitted that it wasn't easy to see how Dolores's *physical* problems could have anything to do with her inner life, but maybe the two of them could look into the possibilities. Dolores agreed, still smiling. As she and Bill discussed recent events in her life, she slowly, reluctantly admitted that her thirty-year-old daughter had divorced her husband and given him custody of their two little boys.

Dolores's inner response to the troubles created by her daughter was this: She believed divorce was forbidden by God, and that her daughter's motives were terribly wrong (she'd chosen to pursue a career and decided her husband and kids were nothing but a hindrance). Another burden she carried was a feeling of disloyalty for sympathizing with Cal and the children, rather than with her own daughter.

It's important to point out that before all this came out in office interviews, Dolores insisted she had no problems of any importance. Life was "just fine." Since she'd long ago resolved to trust God, she had nothing to feel sad about. But as she unloaded her heart's burden, she began to understand the real weight of her many sorrows. Because she misunderstood what faith means, she had not allowed herself to feel, and so her tensions had apparently turned into aches and pains. Though she refused to face the "defeat" of feeling negative emotions, those emotions insisted on facing her!

Many Christians who are hurting (perhaps even in despair) are afraid to admit that they don't have all the answers. Some of us feel guilty for carrying within us this chasm of sorrows because we wrongly believe it means our faith is inadequate. "I can't be spiritual if I feel bad," we tell ourselves. And so we work hard each day to think positively, and above all to look *happy*.

Mask-wearing works for a while. But one of its negative pay-backs is physical tension and even illness, as Dolores discovered. And then dawns that one morning when, as you're washing your face before the bathroom mirror, you catch a glimpse of your own eyes looking back at you, filled with lonely anguish. You can find yourself physically or emotionally *forced* to face reality. But why wait till you are on the brink?

It is not scriptural or mature to pretend that our deep sorrows don't exist. True, they need not cripple us from performing our duties—but to deny them usually only leads to illness, both physical and spiritual. Consider the heartbreak of some of the Bible's best-known fathers and mothers—among them heroes of the faith: Eli's troubles with his sons; David's agony over the handsome and rebellious Absalom. Adam and Eve had a murderous son, Cain; Jacob had lying, incestuous, brother-envying offspring. Samson's love life sickened the hearts of his father and mother, even God the Father anguished over His "son" Israel (see Hosea 11). If God is pained over the sins of His children, why do we think we need to act as though our pain does not exist?

Though each of us thinks, "How incongruous it is that *I* should have to suffer!" reality first begs, then demands that we look it in the face. We need to understand that we cannot go around but must go through our problems. To do so we have to first accept their existence.

Are you one of those avoiders who tries never to think about the story of Job lest you have to confront misery head-on and thus stop pretending your own misery doesn't even exist? If you are, you don't want to see how God permitted, even goaded, the Destroyer into ruining a man whose only crime was his meticulous attention to pleasing God! You don't want to have to think about how Job's wealth, his land, his sons, and his daughters—even his comfort and physical health—were stripped from him. You don't want to admit that we live in a universe where Satan is allowed to molest such a man with pain so excruciating that when his friends came to console him, all they could do was sit silently on the ash heap with him for a week, speechless in the face of such heart-rending agony! Because Job didn't seek to duck the facts of his misery, didn't pretend he felt fine, didn't persuade himself (as many do today) that spiritual forces had nothing to do with what must have been a string of "tough breaks," he comes *through* it victorious! At the end of the dark tunnel, he comes face to face with God! "My ears had heard of you, but now my eyes have seen you." Time to stop burying your pain. With Job, face it. With Job, go *through* it!

When the Scriptures, the measuring rod with which we test the meaning of the events of life, give us plain reasons why we have to go through trials and sorrow, we must remind ourselves that the pain and sorrow we suffer over our offspring are included. Here is a list of the good results you can expect from courageously enduring your child-based miseries:

A personal maturity and completion through perseverance. The apostle James spells it out in chapter 1: "Consider it pure joy, my brothers, whenever you face trials of many kinds, because you know that the testing of your faith develops perseverance. Perseverance must finish its work so that you may be mature and complete, not lacking anything."

A deeper knowledge of God's comfort. Paul asserts that though some pain may be very severe, God "comforts us in all our troubles" (2 Corinthians 1:4). What we suffer now is achieving for us such a massive positive end result that present trials will seem light by comparison (2 Corinthians 4:17, 18).

A clearer faith. Peter assures us that our anguish has

an aim—to purify our faith (1 Peter 1:6, 7).

An eternal inheritance of life. James stresses hanging in there. The promised outcome of all the trouble, to those who persevere, is this: "Blessed is the man who perseveres under trial, because when he has stood the test, he will receive the crown of life that God has promised to those who love him" (James 1:12).[1]

How do we persevere under trial? Again, the Bible can tell us how. Hebrews 12 invites us to take a fresh look at the chasm of remorse—to work our way through it by learning to tell ourselves the truth about it.

> Endure hardship as discipline. . . . No discipline seems pleasant at this time, but painful. Later on, however, it produces a harvest of righteousness and peace for those who have been trained by it. (Hebrews 12:7–11)

According to this passage, trouble does not confirm that we are wretched failures as parents, neither does it mean that God has overlooked us or that He hates us. Rather, it states that our sadness can have a cleansing, sacramental power to refashion us—if we place it in His hands, allowing Him to change and rebuild us from within.

Here are some of the truths, gleaned from Hebrews 12, which you can tell yourself as you face trials:

- No discipline *ever* feels good.
- The pain is for a *time*. It's limited; it will end.
- When I have come through, I will have *learned*.
- I will actually experience a great *harvest of righteousness and peace* by virtue of my "trouble training."

Do you find it hard to endure because it seems as though your prayers for your child are not getting through to God? Even Jesus had the problem of praying

---

[1]The following are more passages of Scripture dealing with the meaning of suffering. Those who want to dwell further on the subject might read Psalm 31, especially verses 14, 15 and 24. See also Psalm 66:8–12; Psalm 34:18, 19; 2 Peter 4:8; Revelation 2:10.

with loud cries and tears and, though God heard Him, He didn't get what He prayed for! (Hebrews 5:7). In the garden of Gethsemane, we find Jesus pleading for a way around the crucifixion. He was so anguished, so full of anxiety, that the droplets of sweat on His brow were actually mixed with blood. But God didn't remove Jesus' sorrow. Instead, in answer to Jesus' prayer, God made Jesus face it and go through it!

The Father calls you to come to Him through your sorrow—not around it, not away from it. If it's sorrow over a child, He invites you to run with endurance the race that is before you, while you fix your eyes on Jesus, the author and finisher of our faith. (See Hebrews 12:2.) God acknowledges that, like Jesus, you too will hurt, you will be fatigued to the point of giving up, you will even pray for escape. And He promises that no matter how demanding and impossible life may seem, *He* will see you through. Ultimately, in a way you cannot now imagine, He will bring you to victory, just as He brought Jesus to the resurrection.

Godly Sorrow vs. Worldly Sorrow

Are you getting the idea that parental problems and trials are unavoidable? Of course, the personal dilemma is that none of us knew they could hurt so bad!

Pain was the element of surprise that almost undid our friends, Jack and Barb, when trouble with their daughter erupted. You may find elements of your own story in theirs. With that hope in mind, we will let Barb relate their experience directly:

"When Karla turned fourteen, mayhem broke loose in our home.

"One terrible day, she turned on me with murderous hatred in her eyes. Her blonde hair had been defiantly tinted pink and green, cut to eyelash length on one side, and 'sharpened' into a set of bright green spikes ominously aimed at the adult world on the other. I had walked into the kitchen to find her slamming gobs of food onto the kitchen floor. Bread and catsup covered broken shards of dinner plates, cups, saucers, and crystal, which she crunched under her feet. Focusing on me coldly, brandishing a ten-inch knife, she said, 'This is what I'm going to kill you with!'

"I waited her out until, finally, she dropped the knife, and left the house, cursing. I was shaken, but a sense of calm came when I decided that *this* time I would have to act. Jack and I had tried so hard to raise Karla according to biblical teachings about right and wrong. How could it have come to this? Until now—perhaps we'd been hiding from our own remorse over Karla—we'd failed to take appropriate action to stop her worsening rampages. Now, to protect ourselves and to get help for Karla, we were forced to file fifth-degree criminal charges against our own daughter! No other avenue remained. Not only had she threatened murder, but her drug habit had progressed to the point where she was selling marijuana to school children. We agonized. What would become of her? Would her fascination with Satanism finally cost her soul? Would she take her own life, as she threatened to do? Would her dropping out of school mean wasting herself on a dead-end job, or worse? For that matter, would Karla ever *hold* a job?

"Jack and I knew the measure was a drastic action, but we telephoned the police.

"The crisis did not end there, however. For the next four years, we were drained emotionally, physically, spiritually and financially. We wondered if we would lose our own sanity as we struggled with every new horror. We learned that it is considered a major fault in our society for parents to have an unmanageable child. We know what it is to feel heartsick with longing for release from sorrow. Even death would have seemed sweet.

"Mere weeks after Karla's first brush with the law, she was at it again, searing us with her hot anger. She got more heavily into drugs; she made a suicide attempt; she ran away from home; she uttered death threats to everyone in the family, especially to me. We stood by, helpless, as our beloved daughter renounced her family and her Lord in exchange for a life of utter sin, with a tough crowd who saw themselves proudly as the most rebellious of all teens.

"At the same time, we felt totally responsible and guilty for what was happening to our child. Whenever she was with us in public, she seemed to us a billboard announcing our utter failure.

"Karla's blonde hair, once thick, had been ruined by repeated dying, ratting and spiking. Her temples were shaved bald, and the top was a mess of hair wadded into thick spikes. Sometimes they were bleached a stark white, sometimes a shocking pink. A white powder covered her once pretty face. She outlined her eyes heavily in black, while her blood-red lips clashed with the deathlike face. She always wore black clothing, usually leather, and usually skintight, seeming to exult in the animal feel next to her body.

"And our home—our once peaceful nest—became a frequent stopping place for the police. We filed runaway reports whenever Karla disappeared for a day or two. Finally, the juvenile authorities took her out of our home. Her behavior was completely out of control. She was breaking things, pounding craters in the floor, gouging holes in the walls, and accelerating her violent verbal outbursts. The last time the police came, Karla was taken out in handcuffs. I was forced to file assault charges against my violent daughter after she beat me with the telephone. Can you imagine our embarrassment as our neighbors peered from their windows at the fiasco our family life had become?

"*Still* it did not stop. Suicide loomed on the horizon. Once Jack had caught her suffocating herself with paint remover, and another time he found her holding a long knife, poised to stab herself in the stomach. Now, she called me at work from the juvenile detention center 'to say goodbye.' She was preparing to hang herself with her bed sheets. Though that crisis was averted, she later tried twice to overdose on Tylenol tablets. A friend in whom she confided called us, and Karla had been found, groggy and lethargic. After treatment in the hospital for severe liver damage, Karla was so suicidal doctors told us we should have her admitted to the psych ward. We were coming to the end of our fraying rope. *How could we help our daughter?*

"Now, unexpectedly, inconveniently, came the last straw. I was pregnant! Daniel was born and we were worried. Karla would stop at nothing in her effort to afflict us. Would she—could she try to harm her baby brother to get even with us? She stoutly denied it, but how could we be sure? When she refused to keep family contracts, we felt we had no choice but to have her removed from our home. We were just plain scared. The only problem was, there was no place to send her.

"Through all this, we sought help. The 'help' wasn't what we had expected. Instead of getting assistance in dealing with Karla, we were blamed. Our family was dissected over and over again by school counselors, social workers, psychologists, psychiatrists, police officers, juvenile court judges and, finally, by our own church friends. Instead of allying themselves with us in an effort to bring Karla to face responsibility for her behavior, counselors and others repeatedly ripped us apart in her presence. The label 'religious fundamentalists' was quickly hung on us, though we are Lutherans, not fundamentalists, in our faith. Because we believed in the judicious use of spanking, we were labeled child abusers. We were told that because our older daughter, Kelly, had not staged a Karla-sized rebellion, she 'had taken the role of parent-pleaser.' This, according to the counselors, left Karla 'no choice' but to be the rebellious child. During one counseling session, a psychologist and a psychiatrist watched our body movements as we talked to one another. After the session, they told us that just from watching us they could deduce a great deal. They knew that if we'd just open ourselves up to Karla, she'd be okay! They explained that we were very nice people, but we just couldn't handle living together because we weren't 'opened up' to the daughter who continually offered us her hatred and contempt.

"At our own church we were stigmatized as 'bad parents.' When we first went to Karla's youth leaders and told them of our concern, they merely shrugged. After Karla's latest overdose and brush with death, our pastor listened politely to our pain, fear, and—yes—anger. Then he suggested I must have some unfulfilled expectations to be so angry! At our fellowship meeting, several people stated that they wouldn't allow this out-of-control behavior in their home. One gentleman suggested that perhaps we'd spent too much time working in the Sunday school program and hadn't given enough time to the girls. A friend stated that God was using this situation to get Jack and me to deal with our own issues so that we would be better parents.

"During this nightmare—to add to our grief—we were judged and condemned by our own relatives. They ripped us apart as terrible parents, insisted that we 'get help for Karla,' accused us of favoring our other children and neglecting her, and briskly rehearsed for us the things we should have been doing. Everyone assured us that if only we would show her enough love, everything would change.

"On top of it all, Jack and I had received some distorted spiritual teaching on 'ancestral bondage.' Hadn't our parents been tainted with divorce and alcoholism? We, as *their* offspring, must be polluted with the same evil, which we passed on to our kids! This put the cap on our utter hopelessness! Supposedly, we were experiencing God's vengeance for our ancestors' crimes, because God was 'visiting the iniquities of the fathers on the children to the third and fourth generations.' But in that case, weren't we all doomed? Jack and I began to withdraw and to participate only in those things we couldn't avoid.

We felt desperate, ashamed and very alone.

"Filing the assault charges took the situation out of our hands. Karla was assigned a probation officer, and he and the judges took it from there. For two years she was shuttled in and out of the juvenile detention center, and between various foster homes. Finally she was placed in a group home out of the city.

"The expenses alone were frightening. The judge looked at our income and expenses and ordered us to take Karla's $750 monthly support payment out of our tithe. The total cost of her various placements came to more than $15,000. And, for us, there was no way out.

"The whole time, Karla was bitter, blamed us, and contrived to keep us on the defensive. She wrote us a letter, stating that *she* had not started this problem; *we* had. Her note was filled with profanities and signed *your unloving ex-daughter.*

"You will probably think that after all this, there was no way to a happy ending. But that's not the case.

"We aren't jumping to any conclusions yet; however, to date, things have become much, much better.

"In the first place, the staff at the Christian group home where Karla was placed forced her to look at her own attitudes and behavior. They also forced her to take responsibility for her actions.

"You may find it miraculous that she has since returned, through repentance and faith, to the Lord! Though there is a long way for us all to go, she is gradually setting her life in order with His help. By God's grace, Jack and I are able to show her the love and encouragement she needs.

"Today, I am able to say that God has brought our devastated family into healing. We're all still in shock and our feelings are often numb. We are scared the improvement won't continue. We find it hard to come out of our emotional hiding places, for fear of further torture. We see that, just as we need God's forgiveness for our failures, we must continually forgive one another.

"Yes, we know what it is to be hunted by the roaring lion 'who roams the earth seeking someone to destroy.' But we know also that the Lion of Judah has already won the battle for us!"

If you are one of those who has had to face your older child's criminal actions head on, perhaps even to the point where you instigated his arrest and/or conviction because it was the only way you could think of to halt his race toward self-destruction, you know the brutal struggle you wage against self-accusing despair.

What Jack and Barb learned to do was to redirect their sorrow until it could work *for* them instead of *against* them. How is this done?

As Barb and Jack studied the Bible with a helpful, sympathetic teacher, they came to understand that not all sorrow must be destructive. Instead, they found two kinds of sorrow: *godly sorrow* and *worldly sorrow.* Eventually, they came to see that they had allowed the devil, the system, and even church members to tell them they were failures, "paying" for their sins. They saw that they had stumbled into a trap; and the way of escape opened before them.

Second Corinthians 7:10, 11 says:

> Godly sorrow brings repentance that leads to salvation and leaves no regret, but worldly sorrow brings death. See what this godly sorrow has produced in you: what earnestness, what eagerness to clear yourselves, what indignation, what alarm, what longing, what concern, what readiness to see justice done. At every point you have proved yourselves innocent in this matter.

Let's look at this more closely.

First, godly sorrow brings *repentance, turning around,* as well as getting a new mind. We want to stress the fact that, while turning *from sin* is important, it is equally important to turn *toward God.* That is, toward His will and empowerment for new life. In other words, godly sorrow can motivate us to turn from sinful, destructive, *self-*

accusations and to live daily with the forgiveness Jesus has won for us at the cross. By the power of the Holy Spirit at work in you, take back control of your life!

Secondly, godly sorrow produces *earnestness*, resoluteness, persistence. It brings a determination to *order* your relationship with your child, instead of a defeatist attitude. It puts to flight an unwillingness to try, and a fear of taking risks for the sake of your love.

Third, godly sorrow also produces *eagerness*. Worldly sorrow saps your energy, leaves you flat, oppressed, wanting only to escape the trouble. The sorrow of real repentance causes you to enthusiastically, ardently pick up the challenge and go to work for *change*. This enthusiasm comes, not from "working it up," but from the energizing power of the Holy Spirit.

Fourth, godly sorrow produces *indignation*. If you're practically squashed into the ground with worldly sorrow, you're too down, too depressed to feel this godly indignation. What the Holy Spirit works in godly sorrow is a godly *outrage*—not at someone else, or at your child, or at God for not doing as you want Him to—but at the principalities and powers and at the worldly and God-hating forces at work in people that have created such havoc in your life. This outrage generates a determination to take up the armor of God and the sword of the Spirit and fight the agencies of sin, death, hell, and family wreckage! Get mad! Get godly mad and go out to battle!

Fifth, Godly sorrow produces *alarm*. The Holy Spirit gives you a jolt! You suddenly wake up out of your nightmare. You sense the spiritual oppression and ask yourself, "What have I been doing here? I've got work to do!"

Finally, a godly sorrow produces a *longing, concern and readiness to see justice done*. Contrast this with worldly sorrow that contents itself with complaining, with distress. Worldly sorrow says, "How awful my lot is! I can't do anything about it. Someone did this to me. God can't help me!" This kind of sorrow produces death, that state of being which is desolate, hopeless and, finally, separated from God.

Of course it hurts when your child won't respond to you, when you have spent the night stewing, unable to sleep as his cutting remarks have bitten into you. It *hurts*, but take control! In your turning around, your repenting, be aware that you are responding to God's call to maturity, and that He will enable you to stand as you work out your salvation.

Sorrow Can Work for You

In Handel's *Messiah*, there is a magnificent section describing the sorrow of Jesus as foretold in Psalm 69 and Lamentations 1. With a sad, haunting accompaniment, the tenor sings, "Thy rebuke hath broken his heart; he is full of heaviness. He looked for some to have pity on him, but there was no man; neither found he any to comfort him. Behold and see if there be any sorrow like unto his sorrow."

Isaiah wrote that our Messiah, the coming King who would give us life eternal, would be a man of sorrows and familiar with suffering. Our lives will, in this respect, be like His. So our question should not be, "How can I have a life in which there will be no sorrow"—but, "How can I become familiar, or acquainted with sorrow *as my Lord was*? How can it be made to work for me to achieve God's will in my life?"

Handel gives us insight. First, his libretto leads us to the fact that God did not leave the Messiah's soul in hell, "nor didst thou suffer thy Holy One to see corruption." No, God brought Him through death to give us hope. When sorrow is unmixed with hope, it's too overwhelming to endure. Then Handel quotes from Psalm 24: "Lift up your heads, O ye gates; and be ye lifted up, ye ancient doors; and the King of glory shall come in. Who is this King of glory? The Lord, strong and mighty, the Lord mighty in battle. The Lord of Hosts, He is the King of glory!"

What this means for us is twofold. First, like Jesus, we can have as a near companion a sorrow or pain for our child that seems to be with us night and day. We don't need to fear the pain, but rather we can embrace it.

At the same time, we can "lift our heads" to see the glory of God as He works, as we acknowledge His power to deliver. Then He will come to us, in the midst of a sorrow too heavy to bear, bringing His peace which passes understanding.

Look up Hosea 11:1–8. Consider God's sorrow over His children. Can you identify with the feelings expressed in this passage?

5

"Forbidden" Feelings

Someone has said making the decision to *have* a child is choosing to have your heart go walking around outside your body. So powerful, so deep is the natural connection with our children that it is virtually impossible to handle their problems with cool, rational objectivity. So it's often true that our natural emotions—our driving desire for a good relationship—becomes a barrier in itself. Since all three inner enemies are emotions rooted at the core of our souls, it's necessary to examine a more basic question: What is your attitude toward *having* and *expressing* emotions? Are emotions *themselves* an enemy or a friend?

Ann's face was as unflinching as stone, and ridged with deep frown lines. Her steely eyes flashed a message you ignored only at your peril: "I'm a private person!" A brilliant woman, a leader in the business world and a teacher in her church, she resisted emotions, good or bad, believing firmly that to feel anything strongly was to risk losing control. It was a mode of living she'd learned long ago.

As a little girl, she discovered the only way to escape the embarrassment of her four brothers' merciless teasing was to stoically conceal frustration and pain. Eventually, it became intolerable to her to be found crying or, conversely, to be caught expressing joy. In her family, emotion was an enemy. It was safer not to allow others any insight into her deeper feelings, because that gave someone grounds to ridicule her. It was safer "not to feel."

It isn't that Ann entertained feelings privately, she *prevented* them from happening. It's true that we all properly *suppress* impulses and emotions at times, as did Ann. But Ann's *repressed* emotions became so buried that they were unknown to her conscious mind. As a result, Ann never understood the joy of a deep friendship, even though she had numerous acquaintances. Her relationship with her husband and children remained duty-oriented and superficial. Though Ann struggled to keep herself sequestered from others emotionally, the feelings she hid from herself were sometimes obvious to almost everyone else.

These masked feelings were known to her body and to others. Ann suffered from arthritis, headaches and psoriasis. It wasn't unusual to find her in bed recuperating from the physical demands of her stuffed emotions. And in her interactions with family, it was not unusual for Ann to attack them or to fall silent, cold and distant. Only Ann, among all the people in her household, would never have described herself as the angry person she was.

Misbeliefs About Feelings

Many of us harbor erroneous ideas about feelings. Some we learned from our parents, some we invented for ourselves as we attempted to explain to ourselves puzzling or painful experiences. Let's examine a few common misbeliefs.

Feeling misbelief #1: *Good people don't have strong emotions and they try not to show feelings if they do have any.*

Ann is not alone. Many people prevent themselves from experiencing at least some of their emotions, beginning with the premise that it's wrong for a "nice person" to have those particular feelings at all. Some cultures have prohibited almost all expression of feelings. Perhaps your nationality or that of your forebears is one where stoicism and reserve are "better" than expressiveness. Some Christians have been taught that it's "not spiritual" to have certain feelings like anger or sadness, and that being led by the Spirit means you don't allow yourself ever to be moved by emotions.

Feeling misbelief #2: *Feelings are bad or at least suspect, so you should never, under any circumstances, trust your emotions.*

Perhaps you are aware of your feelings, but you wish you weren't because you can't trust them. You're uneasy and uncertain about them and what to do with them. Perhaps expressing your feelings has caused a negative reaction from a person of great significance to you—a parent, friend, spouse—so you've "learned" that your feelings, when expressed, can get you into trouble. Moreover, you can never predict when that will happen. So you tell yourself you can't trust your emotions or know what to do with them.

Feeling misbelief #3: *Feelings get in the way of straight thinking.*

Because feelings aren't logical, you believe you shouldn't give them any importance. Feelings get in the way of straight thinking. They aren't logical, so don't give in to them—as if logical thought is all that matters! Many men get into trouble with this misbelief. Perhaps it's due to their *maleness*, to a biochemically conditioned preference men have for sorting things out sequentially and logically. Many women also pride themselves in being logical, thus refusing to allow themselves to have feelings or to accept what has sometimes been called "the logic of the heart." The kind of mind-set that devalues emotions is unfortunate, because feelings give color and dynamic to life. Also, our feelings can often alert us to what we consider most important.

Feeling misbelief #4: *Feelings aren't worth the trouble they cause.*

Have you expressed your feelings to someone, only to wind up in a big fight? Maybe you live with a person who is threatened by emotion—not only his own, but anybody's. So when you've expressed strong feelings, you were rewarded with withdrawal or anger. Have you told yourself that it just isn't worth it and reverted to suppressing your feelings—perhaps even to ignoring them yourself? Has peace at any price become the rule in your household?

The truth is this—even if someone else objects, even if you deplore your feelings, you have them! You are human. Trying to tell yourself not to have emotions is useless, and it invites only trouble in the long run.

Feeling misbelief #5: *Unless you resist, feelings will carry you away.*

Emotions can be so powerful you become afraid of the extent to which they will control you. The most common feeling misbelief that we've encountered in counseling is the terror that if you let yourself feel, you'll lose control of your behavior.

Ann hid her feelings partly because her brothers made fun of her, but also because she feared being carried away with that emotional power hidden inside. Occasionally, she'd experience a surge of love or hate strong enough to break the iron links with which she had trussed up her soul—but when this happened it scared her. She would feel so anxious that she fought until she'd chained her feelings up again. Only then did she feel safe, only then could she let herself think she was in control.

The truth is that feelings won't carry you away unless you let them. People talk about emotions getting out of control, "making" them do things they "can't help." People say, "I was angry enough to kill"—but, in fact, they didn't murder anyone. Even though some people allow their emotions to carry them into actions that are beyond normal limits, most don't go further so as to get into real trouble. And they don't because they, not their emotions, are in control.

The Right to Have Negative Feelings

Many try to deny your right to experience negative feelings. Candy had bought into this kind of denial so strongly we'll let her speak for herself on this issue:

"Neither Bill nor I realized how insecure I became when he expressed anything other than positive feelings. If he was upset about something—even if it had nothing to do with me—I'd become unsettled. I needed his constant assurance that 'everything is okay.' How unrealistic!

"After three years of marriage, Bill one day yelled at me in utter frustration. He'd been feeling down about something and, in my need to reassure myself, the only 'solace' I could offer was to say, 'It's dumb to feel that way.' Bill blew.

" *This* is how I feel, whether *you* think I should or not! It's *my* feelings I'm talking about, not *yours.*'

"I finally got the message. My habit of telling others how they *ought* to feel had to go!"

Why do we try to deny others the right to have negative feelings? Why do they deny us the right? It's usually because some folks feel threatened if the feelings aren't "nice." We become disturbed and fearful and try to protect ourselves.

In the end we are protecting no one—least of all ourselves.

Why Do I Need to Recognize Feelings?

There are several reasons why it is very important for you to recognize and admit feelings, especially as they pertain to difficulties with your child.

The first is to eliminate confusion: to substitute clarity for disordered, bewildered, or mixed up perspectives. Unless you get on speaking terms with your own emotions, you'll continue to be controlled by powerful but *unacknowledged* feelings over which you've drawn a mental curtain. Until you make friends with your feelings, until you and your emotions are on a first name basis, your own actions and reactions will continue to puzzle you and confuse your situation.

Second, feelings add a positive color to life. As a special gift from the Creator, emotions enrich all your other experiences. Would you rather live in a mental desert where all your experiences are drab, bleak and barren? Or in a garden, bursting with freshness and life?

A third reason not to try to curtain off your feelings is that you were made in the image of God. If your idea of God has been shaped by philosophy, you probably think of God as an "it" and not as a Person, as a "force" and not as a Father. But He is a living, self-conscious Lover, with genuine emotions. This is the God revealed to us by our Lord Jesus Christ.

Not only is the true God a feeling Person, He is the inventor of our emotions. It might help you, if you have a problem with feelings, to try listing the feelings ascribed to God in the Bible (or to Jesus, who is God in the flesh). God exhibits a wide range of emotions: love, hate, anger, sadness, joy, sorrow, pain.

The best perspective we can find on divine emotion is the life of Jesus. Of course, He is not only God, He is Man, too. But He is the perfect Man; the whole, complete human Person, so it's helpful to study His walk. The important thing to remember about His feelings is that He let them function constructively, not destructively, even when they were negative. In other words, He made them work *for* Him and for the good of others. They weren't a liability to Him and they were not harmful to others. He acted. He didn't merely react. This important distinction means that, subject to the Father's will, He remained in full control of His own life. No one, He assured people, took His life from Him. Rather, even when it looked like He was helpless under the mighty power of His enemies, in reality, He was laying His life down of His own accord.

When you are walking in the footsteps of Jesus, letting His Spirit work in you, you too can make your emotions work for good, just as He did. Imitate Christ. Keep in touch with your feelings.

How Do I Get in Touch With My Emotions?

For some, discovering their own feelings will be a new adventure. If you've never done it before, you're probably asking how to do it.

Our advice is to go before God in prayer. Make your own emotion-search a prayerful collaboration with God. Choose a time when you can get away from the disruption of everyday life and, in the company of your heavenly Father, discover parts of yourself that are to be—at least for now—for your eyes only.

True, it can be frightening to come closer to yourself, especially if you have not done this for some time. Allow yourself time to think and to explore with your Creator. Consider how you are intricately made, and how He has also fashioned your child—the one with whom you're experiencing heartache. Allow the Spirit of God to reveal *yourself* to you, as *He* sees you, without the customary cover-ups. Just as, in Psalm 42, "deep calls to deep," so let the deep heart of the Spirit of God make contact with your own deep inner self, your genuine feelings and thoughts. Let Him bring forth and reveal what has been hidden.

Getting in touch with your emotions can be likened to solving a puzzle. Here are the four steps: Detect Clues; Find the Underlying Self-talk; Label Accurately; Focus Your Attention on the Result.

Begin the process of gathering clues by letting yourself be creative in describing your present feelings. Describe freely and exactly what you feel in yourself at this moment or at whatever moment you become aware that you're conscious of *something* emotional. Be as creative as you can in how you describe your feelings to yourself before God.

The following list will help if you are at a loss for emotion labels—if you know you're feeling something but need help in finding the right words. Place a check by words that describe your feelings now, as well as you can identify them:

Group one:

_____ Sad
_____ Self-critical
_____ Hopeless
_____ Lethargic
_____ Heavy

_____ Tired
_____ Poor appetite or overeating
_____ Insomnia
_____ Poor concentration
_____ Difficulty making decisions
_____ Feelings of worthlessness or excessive guilt
_____ Significant weight loss or weight gain

Group two:

_____ Nervous
_____ Tense
_____ Jumpy
_____ On edge
_____ Fearful
_____ Restless
_____ Muscle tension, aches, soreness
_____ Shortness of breath, or smothering sensation
_____ Palpitations, or accelerated heart rate
_____ Sweating, or cold, clammy hands
_____ Dry mouth
_____ Dizziness, or light-headedness
_____ Nausea, diarrhea, or other abdominal distress
_____ Flushes, or chills
_____ Frequent urination
_____ Trouble swallowing, or "lump in throat"
_____ Exaggerated startle response
_____ Difficulty concentrating or mind going blank
_____ Trouble falling or staying asleep
_____ Irritability

Group three:

_____ Thinking of getting even with someone
_____ Preoccupied with the badness of someone
_____ Feel like screaming, hitting, slamming
_____ Withdrawal from family or friends
_____ Procrastination
_____ Sulky, irritable, or argumentative

_____ Critical, or scornful
_____ Thoughts of violence or cruelty

Group four:

_____ Short-tempered
_____ Irritable
_____ Bursting into tears
_____ Confused
_____ Thoughts of fleeing or getting away from it all
_____ Agitated
_____ Restless
_____ Disappointed
_____ Insecure

Group five:

_____ Thoughts of having failed someone
_____ Worthless
_____ Rejected
_____ Ashamed
_____ Inadequate
_____ Insecure
_____ Tense
_____ Feels like a sword is hanging over your head
_____ Reluctance to be around God

Group six:

_____ Sorrowful
_____ Concerned
_____ Apprehensive
_____ Sad for someone else

Group seven:

_____ Crying a lot, but not knowing why
_____ Others asking you what is wrong

_____ Fatigue with no physical cause
_____ Headaches
_____ Stomach, or gastrointestinal symptoms
_____ High blood pressure

You may find most of your checked clues are in one or two groups, or you may find that they are more-or-less evenly spread around. If, as is common, most of your checks are concentrated in just a few groups, use the next paragraph to grasp the meaning of your clues when they are taken together:

- If you have checked many items in group one, you may be feeling *depressed*.
- If you have checked many items in group two, you may be *anxious*.
- If you have checked numerous items in group three, you are likely *angry* at someone, or at several persons.
- If you have checked numerous items in group four, you are probably feeling *frustrated* and *stressed*.
- If your check marks are concentrated in group five, you may be troubled by feelings of *guilt*.
- If you focus on group six, you may be feeling *empathy, sympathy* and perhaps a special and *painful identification* with someone else—with your troubled child perhaps.
- If your checks bulk up in group seven, you may be a person who shifts emotion away from mental awareness into *physical signs and symptoms*. This may also indicate that you very much need to become aware of feelings as feelings, and that you need the help of a counselor to do so. Too, it's important to have your physical symptoms evaluated by a physician before you decide that their underlying cause is purely emotional.

Whatever the main emotional thrust, we know that it is vital for you to listen to your *self-talk*. By it, you can identify the nature of your feelings. Say, for instance, your internal monologue is full of ideas similar to the following:

I've really blown it as a parent. If I weren't a terrible person, I wouldn't be having this trouble with my child now. Clearly, I'm inferior, worthless, defective. I wish I'd never become a parent. I never do anything right, so there's no use trying, is there? It won't help—nothing will help. God doesn't care. He doesn't love me. Even if He does, He won't change anything for me. The situation won't get any better. There's no hope. I wish I were dead . . .

Those ideas go with and generate feelings of *depression*. Suppose your self-talk resembles this:

I'm so scared of what's going to happen. I just know things are about to blow up in my face. What then? [You have a list of "what ifs" in your mind, which you can run through over and over again—all the worst events you can think of.] It will be so awful, I couldn't stand it. My heart's pounding, and I feel so tense and jumpy. I just know something dreadful is about to take place. And I'm so helpless and weak. So vulnerable. And what will other people think when they hear about it? I can't face them—I just can't. Oh, I'm getting so nervous I'll probably end up in the hospital over all this . . .

Thoughts like these in your internal monologue generate *anxiety* or *fear*.

Or suppose, when you tune in on your internal speech, you pick up thoughts like these:

It's terrible what's been done to me. I don't deserve it. I know that what so-and-so did was aimed right at me. It's outrageous. He doesn't care about my needs or wishes—it's downright insensitive. Someone ought to have to pay and pay a lot! I'd like to kick someone, or hit someone. I just want to get even . . .

Those thoughts and others like them underlie *anger*. What if your thoughts resemble this monologue:

I can't stand this much longer. I know I'm going to

crack. I just want to leave, to get away. It's getting me down. Whatever I try goes haywire. I just don't know why nothing works out for me. But I'm not going to put up with it much longer . . .

Check to see whether these thoughts are provoking feelings of *frustration*.

As the parent of a troubled or troublesome child, you're also liable to discover thoughts of the following nature in your internal monologue:

It's all my fault. I'm the cause of my child's troubles. He told me it was my poor parenting, and I believe it. Nobody could possibly excuse my failure to bring up my child better. I'm so wrong, and I hate to think of anyone else knowing. Probably my child will never forgive me and I'll never forgive myself. God probably can't forgive me either . . .

These thoughts generate feelings of *guilt*.
Having thoughts like this?

My poor child. I hate seeing him suffer like this. And I worry about him constantly. What chance does my child have? It's like a sword going through my heart when I hear of the things happening to my child.

Such thoughts underlie *sympathetic* and *empathetic* feelings of misery for someone else.

You may not be sure what your internal monologue contains. You probably haven't been paying attention to it because your painful feelings grab all your attention. To really understand how your emotions affect your everyday life, you may need to sort out the variety of ideas and feelings that rummage around in your head by keeping a simple journal or log. This will help you detect, label and focus your emotion.

Divide a notebook page into four columns. Concentrate on one situation and the emotions it generates, perhaps on the child with whom you are having problems. You probably will find numerous internal clues, a variety of thoughts and feelings about this child—memories that make you smile, thoughts that may make you want to cry, even bewildering clusters of contradictory notions. What is important is to allow yourself to have both good and bad emotions regarding him or her.

Let yourself be free right now to simply come to know what these various feelings are. A little later we will teach you how to deal constructively with them. I've included a sample log you may want to use as a model.

Don't worry about doing this "correctly"—the chart simply helps you to understand what you are feeling and why. Can you see how you can learn by sorting out and labeling your feelings? You can make genuine contact with those strange emotions of yours. It is possible to have many *different* feelings about the same situation and the same person. In the case of someone you love, your problem child, the negative feelings can dovetail with and outweigh for the moment your good and positive thoughts and feelings connected with that child. By charting your varied and sometimes opposite feelings, you can look at the situation and take steps to deal actively with each emotion.

Clues	Self-Talk	Label	Focus
Nervous, tense, worried	She's going to move in with her boyfriend. How can she do this to us? To herself? What if she gets pregnant? What if she loses her faith? I'm so worried about her!	anxiety	Suzy
sad, hurt	She'll only be hurt and I know she's doing this because she's hurt already. She feels so bad about herself! I'm so sorry for her! And she's making me feel so bad, I don't see how I can stand it.	empathetic	Suzy
embarrassed chagrin	What did I do wrong? What will I tell God! I really failed. What will others say? I can't face them!	guilt, shame	Self

A Final Word

Getting in touch with your own feelings means, in fact, that you may be getting to know, for the first time, a long-slumbering part of yourself. As you get to know yourself more completely, you will be able to place yourself under the lordship and direction of the Holy Spirit. It is a two-way street of responsibility. You commit your emotional responses to His care; He gives back to you a healthy self-control based on honest, balanced reactions—not stifled emotions or outbursts.

Without question, exposing your feelings to God in a prayer-conversation is the best way to mature emotionally and spiritually. After all, God devised your emotional makeup and He has a use for it. Submitting the full range of your inner makeup to Him may prove to be one of the most intense, meaningful and transforming experiences of your Christian life. You will find, we believe, how much of your life you have based on false beliefs and erroneous messages you give yourself in your internal monologue. Replacing those life-dominating falsehoods with the truth proves to be, for many, one of the most liberating experiences of a lifetime.

As Jesus has promised, "You will know the truth, and the truth will set you free" (John 8:32). Perhaps freedom—from fear, anger, remorse, and other related emotions—is something you never thought you'd feel again. Regardless of your child's future, regardless of his or her choices, freedom is God's will for you.

Why not begin to get free today? God is standing at your side right now, waiting to gently, lovingly help you face the inner burdens you've been carrying.

Take some time to pray.

Do you suspect you have feelings you're not in touch with? If so, what might they be? If not, ask God to reveal them to you. Check the following psalms. See how the

psalmist openly discusses his tears with God. Psalm 6:6; Psalm 39:12; Psalm 42:3; Psalm 56:8. Now check these verses to see the outcome you can expect from your tears. Psalm 116:8; Psalm 126:5.

6

Denial: Walking in Darkness

In one sense it was a professional family. The father, mother and two daughters were professional *deniers*, skilled at maintaining a state of denial in themselves and in one another. They locked the doors of consciousness on what was true. It was the way they stayed alive. They knew of no other way to cope with the crises created by Mother's drinking. They couldn't bring themselves to use the word *alcoholism*. Mother had drilled them well. Everyone learned to repeat: "Yes, she sometimes drinks a little too much. But only because Dad is never home and she gets lonely."

True enough, Dad was away from home on business for most of each week—a nice break for him from the increasingly bizarre struggles of his wife and two little girls. Kathy, the older sister, immersed herself in school achievements, pulling down high grades to compensate for her misery at home. Little Janey pretended a lot. She made believe life was fun, so nothing was hurting. With her warm laughter, sparkling eyes and zest for touch football with the neighborhood kids, she played in order to forget her rejection, fear and irrational guilt. Mom—she drank away her loneliness and her days.

None of them knew the fundamental Reality, the Father of Jesus Christ. Nor had they discovered His tender, powerful love. How then could they dream that over the next twenty-five years He would work to reverse the devastations they were trying to handle by playing games with life?

One day, Mom nearly died in a dangerous state of alcohol withdrawal. In her panic, she cried out to God.

Perhaps in answer to her prayer, she wound up in an Alcoholics Anonymous group. There, she was instructed and encouraged by fellow sufferers. She learned to fight her disease while, in the power of the Holy Spirit, she fought her own sinful contribution to the problem.

But it wasn't that easy. Two years later, the family that had weathered the storm of alcoholism was shattered by the stresses of recovery. Now that reality began to break through the curtains of denial pulled down in front of it, Mom and Dad divorced.

Dad moved to another city. Kathy went off to college and handled the latest evil by falling back on her old friend—denial. But sixteen-year-old Janey was devastated as she went off, numb, to live in a hotel on Waikiki Beach with her mother. Mom and Janey never imagined that what they were about to encounter would make alcoholism seem tame by comparison.

Janey began to feel rebellious. Something like anger kept gnawing at her—though she had no idea whom she was mad at. Feeling destructive and vengeful (toward whom, she didn't know), she became pregnant by the son of her mother's best friend. If she was trying to express rebellious anger at her parents, Janey couldn't have found any more effective way. They'd taught her from childhood that sex outside of marriage, especially sex that made babies, would never be tolerated. Terrified for her, they now offered only two solutions: give the baby up for adoption or abort it.

"How could you do this to me, Janey?" her mother screamed one afternoon. She promptly poured herself a drink—the first she'd mixed since turning her back on alcohol.

A dramatic contest of wills ensued. Janey threatened to

jump from their 16th floor balcony if her mother touched the drink. Mother and daughter glared at each other in a standoff. The devil laughed—but the Father in heaven laughed last, for He saw it all, and patiently waited for the right moment to reveal His victory.

The crisis passed when Mom poured her drink down the sink—but in both mother and daughter feelings of rejection and condemnation swirled. They hated each other; each hated herself.

As the days passed, Janey couldn't eat or sleep. Her weight fell to 85 pounds. Her mother, smarting under the blows of her pride, looked at her with coldness. Janey was sure her mother hated her. It made sense, didn't it? She was evil for having "gotten" pregnant.

Worst of all would be her grandmother's reaction. This gracious, southern lady—refined, proper, proud—what would she say? "What will Nana think of me if she finds out?" Janey berated herself.

Janey went out to lie on the beach where the big waves could wash over her. Maybe somehow the pounding surf smacking against her little body would dislodge the wretched, unwelcome little life growing inside her—"the little one" who, in spite of everything, Janey already loved.

She was never to touch or hold her child. Japan was the place to go for an abortion in those days. No one would condemn her, nor would her action be looked upon as a crime in Japan. A quick trip to Japan, and Janey and her parents could deny that anything ever happened. Almost. Deep inside, they all knew they were choosing to sin.

The hospital in Tokyo was clean but primitive. Day and night, the halls were scrubbed with a strong-smelling disinfectant. The nurses made Janey scrub from head to toe with the stuff when she and her mother arrived.

Janey would never erase from her memory the image of the doctor in his blood-stained coat, never forget the horror of being tied to the operating table with ropes and rags. The ultimate humiliation was the doctor's assumption that she must have been promiscuous, probably a prostitute. He asked her whether she had syphilis or gonorrhea, because only victims of venereal diseases came to his hospital for abortions.

Janey lay on the table, feeling dirty, alone, ashamed, and utterly rejected. Succumbing to the sodium pentothal, she felt sure she was drawing her last breath. And though she didn't know Him, she asked God for mercy.

Following Janey's ordeal, and true to their lifelong habit, the family handled her abortion by never even discussing it. It was as if it had never happened. Though they had all come to know Jesus Christ as their Savior and Lord, and knew that He would one day bring each of them face to face with their past sins in repentance and faith, they had not yet learned all that He teaches about bringing buried issues to the light.

God was working in all of them in different ways to lead each one to the point where living out His truth included coming right out into the light, to replace their timeworn denial tactics with real healing and certainty of forgiveness.*

Janey's mother grew as a Christian, and even learned how to minister to the sick and the sorrowing. Through her witness, many people came to know the saving power of Jesus Christ. She drew from all the resources she knew: the power of the Holy Spirit, her master's degree in counseling, and her own gift of compassion. But her own need for healing stubbornly resisted all attempts to make a victorious spiritual assault on it! Why?

Years passed.

Kathy, the older sister, now the divorced mother of a nine-year-old girl, began to question what had shaped the person she was, and the person her little sister was. So it was that, for the first time in twenty-five years, the sisters

---

*In John 3:19–21, Jesus' instruction on this issue yields a principle: The truth is something to be *lived* or *done*, not merely grasped intellectually. And when people become intensively involved with His truth, they will no longer try to cover and hide their deeds, but will bring them to light in order that they may be rightly evaluated as being of God or not of God. In other words, "Don't use repression and denial as hypocritical coverups, but open up and let the light of God's truth pass judgment on your real motives and actions."

ventured out of the darkness together with Jesus as their Guide. They actually talked honestly. They spoke about the alcoholism and the divorce in their family. They assessed the ways each had been affected.

Both Kathy and Janey found it terrifying and exhilarating to be held in the hand of the living God. At first Janey wanted to keep the past hidden. Helped by the hiding, she had compartmentalized the people in her life, neatly tucked a safe distance away like important papers that were seldom looked at, locked up out of sight. Little did she know that freedom and restoration were ahead for her and her family.

It was Mom's honesty that finally broke through the walls of denial—honesty that was hard-bought. Arthritis in her hip continued to worsen despite the prayers of many. She was perplexed and frustrated. Finally the physical pain, crippling debilitation, and the hip-replacement surgery she could no longer avoid forced her into a position of great vulnerability. Slowly, she faced her own physical pain, and at the same time she allowed her emotional pain from the divorce and the alcoholism to come into the light. She dared both to look herself in the face and to put herself in her daughters' shoes, feeling what they must have felt through the years.

Then Mother did the unthinkable. She actually *talked* to her grown daughters about all that had wounded them so many years ago! She even asked them to express to her all of their frustrations, to recount her faults and failures, past and present, as they experienced them. She trembled with fear! She recoiled again and again from the process. It was by far the hardest thing she had ever done. The agony of the surgery that took place in her soul was much worse than the pain left in her hip from the surgeon's chisel and hammer. But she got through them both, opening up new doors and windows for the light to stream into her relationships with her daughters and herself.

When Mom came home from the hospital after her operation, Janey came for a visit. It began to dawn on her that Mom had changed. There was a quiet dignified humility which replaced the old defensiveness. There was a peace about her, and a beautiful, free spirit.

What a threat! Janey knew very well how to be polite to her mother while remaining aloof. Emotionally she had rejected her mother the way she thought she had been rejected by her. It had been too dangerous to get close, for she never knew if she'd be accepted or rejected. So while Janey had perfected her own veneer of impeccable behavior, beneath it, she seethed with anger. Long ago she had willed herself to forgive her mother, her father and herself for the abortion, but now there was much more to deal with . . . things that Janey had kept in the darkness, things her mother had kept in the darkness. Her sister Kathy encouraged Janey to open up, reminding her how fierce is a mother's love.

With Understanding Comes Forgiveness

After an intense struggle, Janey opened up. For the first time in twenty-one years, mother and daughter talked about the horror of Janey's abortion, which had so long kept them at emotional odds.

Janey had always taken full responsibility for the pregnancy and the abortion, acknowledging that she had sinned grievously through her own fault. She knew that it wasn't the divorce or her mother's drinking that had caused her to rebel, but her own stubborn sinful nature that had willed what she knew was wrong. It was not her mother's or her father's fault, it was her own. What she'd never faced was feeling rejected by her own mother. But as they began to talk, Janey finally saw the dawning light—just a spark at first, then the radiant, blinding light of understanding. Janey now understood that, instead of rejecting Janey, her mother had felt deep horror at what had happened—and for twenty-one years she'd hidden it in the dark, unable to force herself to talk about it. Putting herself in her mother's shoes, Janey also realized the guilt her mother had felt when the Japanese doctor showed her the aborted remains of her own grandchild.

From that day, the relationship turned around. Janey—never free of the grief of ending her baby's life—had been certain she was alone in her sorrow, because she and her mother had never once spoken of what was going on inside. She'd never known that her mother was suffering with her.

Nine months after the first breakthrough, a letter from Mom arrived. With trembling hands, the daughter read her mother's salutation: "Candy Dear"—for you see, "Janey" was really a nickname, one Kathy had given Candy many years ago when they played in their fantasy world. "Candy Dear" meant that it was going to be an intense letter.

Though Candy's mom had asked forgiveness for what she'd done, she was now asking to be forgiven for her deeper, sinful attitudes. She confessed her failure, her pride, her coldness. She acknowledged that she should have held, cuddled and loved Candy when she was young and pregnant. She confessed that she'd made terrible choices, condemning her to a life of fears and guilt. She was not seeking to be forgiven for her sake—to relieve her own guilt, for that had already been accomplished. She wanted forgiveness for Candy's sake—and for their relationship in Christ.

Here was courage! Real vulnerability. What if Candy rejected her now, because of these new sins that she was exposing? She was willing to risk that possibility, desiring instead to set Candy as free as possible after long years of despair. At last, she was taking her proper role as mother and protector, initiating a healing. She was offering to lay down her life for her daughter. Candy will tell the rest.

"In that letter, Mom also gave me hope! She did it by painting a picture for me of my beloved Nana, now in heaven, holding and comforting 'our' baby. Surprised by joy, I kept gazing at this word-picture with the eye of imagination. More priceless to me than a Rubens or a Rembrandt, it meant powerful truths, for it said, 'I accept and love your baby, my grandbaby, and one day we will both hold our "little one" too!'

"Of course I forgave Mom—and when I did, the powers of darkness that for years had been preserved by despair began to dissipate. An important new truth took root in my heart: My mother, a sinner like me, had done the very best she could have done at the time.

"Vulnerability and forgiveness are powerful things! The result of all this is a new relationship that is filled with the utmost respect. My mom continues to walk in freedom, ministering grace, healing and freedom wherever she goes. And I live in the security of knowing a faithful, restoring God, who never ceases to show mercy."

There are several valuable lessons that we learned from Candy's mother. They can help you tremendously as you learn to walk away from the darkness as a parent.

First, *treat your child as an equal, not like an immature adolescent*. This one is not as easy for parents as it might sound.

Candy's mother saw Candy as having value. Can you imagine how a teenager feels as she views her parents looking down in a condescending way? Can you imagine how that child feels, being raised up to new heights, valued for her ideas and feelings? To be counted the same as her parents in sinfulness and in righteousness? To be held up to face a new challenge with her parents, knowing that she can indeed face that challenge, that she has all that it takes, that they have confidence in her?

Second, *she managed, by the Holy Spirit, to put herself in Candy's shoes*. She got so far out of her own skin that she thought and felt like her daughter. Because she no longer was spending valuable time defending herself, or manipulating her daughter into feeling a certain way, her attitude changed completely. She accepted her daughter just the way she was, good and bad, frail and strong. By this one act, she revolutionized their relationship.

Third, *she took control of the relationship and turned it around by letting herself be vulnerable first—when vulnerability was most frightening*. She risked her life for her daughter. So often we wait for the other person to make the first move. Then and only then will we follow. While anyone in a relationship *can* make the first move toward restitution, all along it is the parents' proper job to teach their young.

The secret is exercising the will, not waiting for your

emotions to indicate when the time is right.

Fourth, *she humbled herself to ask for forgiveness.* She knew restitution would be neither cheap nor trite. Remembering Proverbs 15:33, she acknowledged that "honor comes only after humility." She realized she had absolutely nothing to lose in asking forgiveness, for her life had already been lost to Jesus Christ, the Caretaker of her soul (see John 12:25).

Fifth, *she rested in the Lord.* The most difficult of all tasks is doing something you know is constructive and then having to *wait* to see the results. Candy's mother waited patiently for the Lord to work in her daughter's life. As she relinquished her daughter to the care of her heavenly Father, she rested by the still waters—ever hoping, ever praying, ever dreaming of a healed relationship.

Sinful motives kept Janey and her mother apart. List Janey's sinful motives. List her mother's sinful motives. List the things each did right to heal the relationship.

7

The Miracle of Vulnerability

Life taught most of us, *eons* ago, that basic survival requires a tough defense. How can you protect your "rights" if you become vulnerable to ruthless attack? Haven't you already given it a try? Hasn't your own experience with your problem child proved to you that being open and vulnerable is only an invitation to be hurt?

So, you're saying to yourself, "Why should I become vulnerable? I can't take it anymore. I have to draw the line."

Drawing a New Kind of Line

There is some truth, of course, in what you are feeling. There is no point in being such a passive punching bag that you effectively train your child to clobber you. A line must be drawn, but it's not the line of withdrawal or defensiveness. Vulnerability doesn't mean that. Although Jesus has often been portrayed as a doormat with a halo, He was nothing of the sort. He asserted, "No one takes [my life] from me, but I lay it down of my own accord" (John 10:18). He gave himself of His own free will. What kind of power was this?

If you have been hurt repeatedly, it's natural to develop a "fortress mentality." You build barricades around the inner self so thick nothing can enter to hurt you again. Survival, you believe, depends on staying safely inside impenetrable walls. Handling fear, guilt, and remorse begins to tear down those walls, setting you on the road to a fresh beginning. The next step is to learn the power that lies in godly vulnerability.

The "Miracle"

"Candy, I hate the way I feel. But I have to tell you—I *hate* my own father more." Twenty-three-year-old Cliff cringed as he spoke openly thoughts he'd never before put into words. "I know you aren't supposed to say you hate anyone—but you *did* ask about my feelings toward my father."

Candy said nothing, and waited for him to go on.

"Dad was there, but *not* there. Always around physically but absent emotionally," Cliff continued. "He pretty much left me alone. When we did talk, Dad kept it superficial. He never got down to nitty-gritty things with me. It's as if he didn't want to get too close.

"And there was never any disagreeing with Dad. He was always right. He thought I was pretty worthless, I guess. Maybe he disliked me on account of my leg." Cliff glanced at his misshapen left leg, the result of an injury he'd suffered at age three. Tears welled up in his eyes as he whispered, "I don't think my father loved me!"

After a few months of misbelief counseling—which Cliff pursued eagerly, with considerable improvement in mood and sense of worth—Candy suggested it might be time to involve his dad. Cliff swallowed hard, expecting the worst. But he agreed, skeptically, that if his father participated in a few sessions it might at least bring things to a head.

Don, his father, seemed relieved to be invited. His first visit with Candy was private. He had a very different story to tell about his relationship with Cliff.

"I was thrilled when Cliff was born. We'd wanted kids

and prayed for a child for several years, so he was a godsend. He was the cutest little guy you ever saw. He was always cheerful in spite of his impairment, even when he couldn't do things the neighborhood kids did. He'd ask me, 'Will I ever be normal, Daddy? Will other kids always treat me this way?' It tore me apart when other children made fun of him.

"Inside, I wanted to protect him—but there was no way. I knew he'd have to take care of himself. So I thought I'd make him stand up for himself, be tough, handle the bad guys. I think that was a mistake, but it seemed right at the time. So I purposely left him on his own. Purposely forced him to depend on himself.

"I can see now that I was protecting myself, too. It was so hard to face him—to try to handle his bewilderment, to answer his unanswerable questions. When I had to be home, I kept myself busy. I know that was just a way of escaping Cliff's pain. I even thought several times about ending all of our lives. I guess Cliff doesn't think too much of me, and I don't blame him. I don't think too much of myself. Can my son and I ever have a good relationship?"

Candy, almost too deeply touched to speak, could only say, "Why don't we find out?"

"I don't know if I can handle facing him," Don answered, "but I'll give it a try. It's as if I've spent twenty years acting a role in a play. Where do we begin?"

Don had taken the first step without realizing it. He was willing to take a serious look at himself and admit to flaws and sins, a frightening challenge for anyone. And he was willing to risk offering to get close to his son. What if it didn't work? What if Cliff were to slam the door on him? Don had turned a corner, though. He was resolved that, whatever Cliff's response, he would no longer defend himself with isolation.

You probably won't like the idea of becoming vulnerable at first. Webster's meaning of "vulnerable" is daunting: *Vulnerable = being open to criticism or attack; capable of being wounded either physically or emotionally; open to assault by armed forces.* As Don went on to learn, it can mean being

willing to suffer at the instigation of your child. Cliff did
not break down weeping in his father's arms. There was no
"Hollywood" ending. At first, the conversations were tense,
then angry. But, as we've said, the way *out* of a problem is
the way *through* it. Today, while they are still building a
relationship, Cliff and Don spend more time together and
enjoy each other's company. They care about each other.
They've learned how to stop hurting each other. All major
steps.

It's also true, however, that Don was greatly tempted to
withdraw when Cliff's anger flared. The same may be true
for you. But before you pull back into your shell for protection or don your heavy armor of self-justification and excuses—think of what life can be like if you don't withdraw
but stay in the line of fire *under the mighty protection of God.*
What could this attitude do for you and for your child?

"Be Like Him"

Psychologists have studied the phenomenon of *modeling*
pretty thoroughly, proving over and over again that for good
or ill, people do what they see others do. Copying the actions of others appears to be an inborn human disposition.
If the model acts immorally or inconsiderately, we may imitate it anyway, especially when we see the model rewarded.
If our chosen model's behavior is constructive, masterful,
kind and loving, we'll imitate that, too.

Jesus, the Son of God, has come to be, among other
things, our *model.* As Peter says: "To this you were called,
because Christ suffered for you, leaving you an example,
that you should follow in his steps" (1 Peter 2:21). And God
has given us a record of Jesus' life, showing one example
after another of how to give, how to serve, how to be pure,
how to love, how to be forgiving, just, and truthful.

What really stands out in Jesus' life is that He knew how
to be *vulnerable.* He never naively expected to be treated
favorably but, knowing the end of it all, He allowed himself
to become the target of hatred, all the while trusting himself to the Father's care. Though He experienced death, the

end result was triumph—*resurrection*.

As hurting parents, we can find new life, too, in following His example. As we open ourselves to the risk of more hurt, in fact, we most often find renewal in our relationships with problem children. The secret is this: *You must become willing for God to do whatever He wants to do in you. You must become willing to do whatever God is asking you to do, even to the point of being willing to lay down your life.*

No doubt you're wondering how—how can you ever become courageous enough to open yourself to hurt, rejection, self-sacrifice? Only through the power released by Jesus' vulnerability. This is a major step. It's important to see that Jesus, too, wrestled with worries, insecurities, and doubts, not only with us, but for us. His anxiety, wounding, beating, and crucifixion were not merely behaviors for us to model, they also accomplish for us and in us what willpower alone could never do. By dying for our sins, He obtained forgiveness for us and opened the way for the Spirit of God to come and empower us to be as vulnerable as He was. Believe Him, trust Him, and go forward.

Having opened up to God, exactly how do you go about being vulnerable with other human beings?

To Be Vulnerable Is to Forgive

"But I can't *forgive* Jerry. That's ridiculous. If you knew him, you'd see what I mean! He'll think he can get away with what he did. He'll just come back and rip me off again. Maybe I'll consider forgiving him when I see some evidence that he's changed."

"Forgive her? Without getting even? No way! I'm not letting her get away with what she did, absolutely not!"

"I'm too angry to forgive that boy. I'm sorry, but I just can't pretend I don't have feelings. I'm no 'plaster saint.' "

Perhaps you have never gotten hold of the truth that forgiveness is an action. You might have come to believe forgiving another is a long process, that it means having nothing but amiable feelings toward the person who's hurt you—therefore, it has to wait until your anger has simmered down. On these terms, it can take weeks, months, or even years to forgive. But Scripture knows nothing of a "process" forgiveness. Even the perfect prayer asks God to forgive us "as we forgive those who sin against us." Jesus goes on to explain that if we don't forgive others, God doesn't forgive us, so when we haven't forgiven someone, we are actually praying in this petition that God will not forgive us!* We are asking Him to delay forgiving us until we have gotten all through with our negative feelings! A dangerous prayer, the Lord's Prayer, for those who plan to delay forgiving another until they feel good toward that person!

Strip away defenses, strip away all arguments about who's really right, strip away fears of consequences, strip away the fuss over feelings, and get down to bedrock: *The essence of forgiveness is not a feeling, it's a deed.*

Forgiving another person is an act of the will. You make a deliberate decision to let the other person off the hook, a decision to battle the impulse to get even, a decision to give up resentment and anger, a decision to be vulnerable.

In some ways, forgiveness is the legal act of making a contract. When you signed your mortgage you might have had some fears that you wouldn't be able to make all those payments. You might have had some hesitation about the extent of your vulnerability in case of default. But when you signed the paper you executed a contract that stands up in court *no matter how fearful you were and no matter whether you really felt good about it or not.* Like executing a mortgage, forgiving your child constitutes a contract that remains valid regardless of your fears or angry feelings.

You might be thinking, "But if that's all forgiveness is, I need only to solemnly tell God I forgive and it's done, whether I feel like it or not!" That's right. That's the essence of a contract. It stands, because you agreed to it. And your forgiveness will be real and valid, too. The following are some "clauses" in the forgiveness contract.

Feelings follow fact. Feelings are not the essence of for-

---

*Matthew 6:14, 15.

giveness. They will follow the act. Maybe not immediately. Maybe not for a long time. But, eventually, your feelings will catch up. Meanwhile, feelings must not be confused with deeds and allowed to stand in the way of the forgiveness act.

Why you should forgive your problem child. Most parents love their problem children so much they want to forgive no matter what the child has done. But maybe you're so angry you've lost sight of any positive feelings for your child. Why should you forgive? Because God wills it. If you can't find any other reason, forgive your child out of simple obedience to God. Forgive your child because you love God. Forgive your child because you want to pray and be heard. Forgive your child because you want to be on good terms with your own Father in heaven.

Forgive instantly and constantly. Keep this phrase in mind. It will remind you that your act of forgiveness remains valid so you can't take it back. When feelings of resentment or thoughts of revenge come sneaking into your internal monologue, beat them back instantly with self-talk like this:

> I have forgiven my child for that, so I am resolved not to keep kicking a dead horse by telling myself how terribly I've been treated. I can do this because I'm willing to be vulnerable and open and to trust myself to the hands of God.

This tactic makes your act of forgiveness a benchmark, a point of reference. When it's done it's done. It's as much a fact as your mortgage. Your once-for-all act of forgiving is a reality you can incorporate into your self-talk to cool your anger and resolve your feelings toward your offending child. All you need to do is maintain your "forgiveness contract" by "making payments" in the form of truthful self-talk whenever angry vindictive thoughts come. This way, forgiveness will no longer be construed as a *result* of positive feelings but a *cause* of them.

Forgive actively. To forgive an offender means to deliberately refuse to treat him as he deserves to be treated—to reject the impulse to get even—to "show him what it's like," to "put him in his place." When you give all that up in an act of forgiveness, you're acting just like God. Think over and over about what God's forgiveness of your sins is like. Here is a psalm fragment that captures the essence perfectly:

> He does not treat us as our sins deserve, or repay us according to our iniquities. For as high as the heavens are above the earth, so great is his love for those who fear him; as far as the east is from the west, so far has he removed our transgressions from us. (Psalm 103:10–12)

Don't put off forgiving. Protective barriers have a way of raising themselves again. Here are some common reasons for not forgiving:

- Refusing or delaying forgiveness is often, at bottom, a frightened attempt to remain invulnerable.
- We want to punish the offender with our unforgiveness—make him suffer.
- We fear change. ("I've finally become comfortable with everything just the way it is! Let's not stir up trouble by bringing distasteful things to light. I might have to change, and I hate change.")
- Or, "If I forgive, then I'll have to try to resume a relationship with him—and I'd really rather keep him at a distance."
- Sometimes it just plain feels good when others are sorry for us. If we forgive, we remove our grounds for claiming sympathy.
- "She doesn't *deserve* it," we may insist—mistakenly believing we derive any benefit by carrying a grudge.

Where does the power to forgive come from? Many insist, "I *can't* forgive. I just *can't.*" If you tell yourself you *can't* forgive your child, you need to refocus your faith on Jesus Christ, the Source of all power to do what we ourselves are too weak to do.

Make sure your focus is pinpointed on His cross, the

means by which God forgives us and empowers us to forgive others. As Paul puts it so graphically,

> [God] forgave us all our sins, having canceled the written code, with its regulations, that was against us and that stood opposed to us; he took it away, nailing it to the cross. And having disarmed the powers and authorities, he made a public spectacle of them, triumphing over them by the cross. (Colossians 2:13–14)

Do you see the principle? When God forgives us through Christ's cross, the devil loses power over us. In the very same way, when we forgive one another, we do it by returning to the cross. The cross of Jesus now mightily disarms those paralyzing, interfering principalities and powers that have been crippling us and our relationship with the offender. We are now free from the heavy burden of the other's unforgiven transgressions and are newly enabled to lay down our lives in love for the other for the sake of Jesus Christ.

"Forgiveness is one thing—*trust* is another!"

"I guess you've got a point about forgiveness—but I don't know if I can trust him again," said Joanne, a forty-five-year-old widow whose struggles with her son were long and difficult. Rich, a college dropout, had repeatedly "borrowed" money from his mother. He had lied, saying that he was using it to pay for job training, while, in fact, he spent Joanne's money on drugs. Joanne, whose resources were meager, would probably never see a penny of her money. Like most people, Joanne believed that forgiveness requires you to *trust* the other person.

Her counselor explained that when you forgive someone, you don't have to trust him. While forgiveness must be given freely, trust must be earned. He instructed her to say to Richard the next time he wanted to wheedle money out of her: "Son, I love you and I forgive you for what you've done, but I don't trust you. I cannot trust you again until you repay what you've taken from me."

Joanne decided to try what her counselor suggested. Richard was shocked at the change in his mother. He tried to pour on the guilt, accusing her of being hard and unloving. "If you were a real Christian, you'd trust me," he accused. Joanne didn't budge.

To trust someone means to have an assured reliance on the character, ability, strength or truthfulness of that person. Once trust has been broken in a relationship, it can take a long time before you regain confidence in that person's character. You cannot make yourself trust someone who has given every evidence that he is not to be trusted. Only changed behavior patterns can rebuild shattered trust. So forgive—but be wise.

Doing vs. Being

At this point, you can decide to go in one of three directions: You could say to yourself, "These people don't know how awful my relationship with my son is. What they're saying won't work for me." Or, you might tell yourself, "All right. I'll forgive my daughter. She doesn't deserve it, but I'd better do it. I don't want to have my prayers rejected. I'll forgive her, but I don't plan to go any further than God's rules require!" What we hope you'll resolve is to choose this third route: "I'll be more than forgiving—I'll *be* that open, vulnerable, forgiving, God-trusting person I'm reading about. I'm going all the way."

We hope you'll decide to *do* the forgiving God requires of you, and to *be* a new, vulnerable person. His strength *will* be perfected in your weakness.

Candy once taught on the value of forgiveness and vulnerability at a women's retreat. She chanced to overhear some of the conversations of participants during the weekend. Here is part of an overheard discussion between Marge and Annie:

> *Marge:* I enjoyed that teaching on how to forgive. It's pretty much what I tried to do when my Kate told me she was pregnant and was having an abortion

and it was just tough if I didn't approve. It wasn't easy "walking the walk" as a Christian, but it helped our relationship. How about you, Annie? Have you ever forgiven your son Jimmy?

Annie: I thought I had. I made a conscious effort and exercised my will to the hilt. I guess I forgave Jimmy and it was real, but now I wonder if I followed through to live it—to "walk the walk" as you put it.

Marge: What do you mean?

Annie: I've been reminded of some things I *haven't* done. For one thing, I determined that I'd never allow Jimmy to hurt me again. By reminding myself of how painful it was, I've kept him at arms' length. When he moved into his girlfriend's apartment, I just about died! I couldn't get it off my mind—what other people would think of us, what the people at church would say, and how thoughtless he was acting toward his family. I knew I had to forgive him. I *did* forgive him. But I wonder if I only *half* forgave him.

Marge: How in the world can you only half forgive someone?

Annie: If I take an honest look at myself, I see that I still have some things to work on here. I've been *doing,* but not *being!* I *did* forgive Jim, but I haven't *been* quite as warm and cordial as I could be. Instead, I've been just a little cool so he'll notice that things aren't quite right but without being able to put his finger on anything in particular. I invite him for dinner, like always, but I make a point of never serving his all-time favorite "volcanoes," a concoction he and I invented when he was five. He loves it to this day! See, I've *done* what was required of me—obeyed the "law"—but I haven't *been* what I should have been, open and vulnerable.

Annie, who was willing and ready for the light of God to uncover attitudes she'd kept in the dark, now realized that *being* vulnerable goes along with *doing* the act of forgiveness. That weekend, she glimpsed the truth. She realized that if she remained inside her emotional fortress, she would never experience the delightful abandon of standing fully out in the open—safe, because of God's protection.

Face-to-Face With Reality

Sometimes the truth that makes us free is the very truth we've been covering up because it's painful. Jesus encourages us to confront the truth in all circumstances, for it's in accepting hard truth that we come face-to-face with reality.

Jesus, the living Word of God, comes to light up the darkest corners of your life. "In the beginning was the Word, and the Word was with God and the Word was God. . . . In Him was life, and that life was the light of men. . . . The true light that gives light to every man" (John 1:1–9).

When His light begins to shine, we may panic and run away from it, knowing full well that it's the searchlight of our souls, and that it can reveal ugliness we don't want to see. But according to the Scriptures His light is our life, our only hope of freedom from death, misery, and the murky waters of self.

When the "Hound of Heaven" was pursuing Candy, calling her to life with Him, she first tried to satisfy His demands while continuing to do what her flesh desired. So she allowed the Lord to ride along in the backseat of her life, imagining with her back to the Lord that He wouldn't see the things she was hiding up front. But He did see. And He let her know. The revelation broke through one day as she read Psalm 139: "O Lord, you have searched me and you know me . . . you are familiar with all my ways." Suddenly those words became *life* to her, and she saw how foolish she'd been. God knew about those things she'd been hiding from Him. It was He who had made her, who knew her before she ever was, and who still knew her through and through!

To a much lesser degree, others *can* see us for what we really are—especially those hawk-eyed people we call our children. They know the difference between a life that is open, reflecting the light within, and one that crosses its arms in front, saying, "Keep your distance!"

If you want a life open to the light, a life lived face-to-face with God, take the leap. Willingly relinquish your "right" to total privacy and stand vulnerable before your Creator, fully aware that your sins are crimson, that in yourself there is no good thing—knowing, nevertheless, that your sins have been wiped away to be remembered no more. Now you have been clothed with a robe of righteousness.

Then, stand with no pretenses before your children. Does one of them criticize you? Try being open to what they have to say, knowing you're a sinner and they might very well have a point. Has one of them blown it badly—sinned against you, burdened you? Forgive, and get on with rebuilding those fragile relationships. Let down your self-protective defenses and pretenses and be what you are—someone who fails, and yet, is loved by God.

When you come to the place where you have nothing to hide and nothing to prove, you'll have a strength made perfect in weakness. A strength that can help repair broken relationships with those you love most.

What do you fear the most about being open and vulnerable to your child? See Mark 11:25, 26.

8

Letting Yourself Go Free

Living in freedom and coping with reality are two sides of the same coin. We have looked at what it takes to deal with your child in *reality.* Now we need to understand how to walk together in *freedom.*

As a Christian, you've heard Paul's cry to press on toward the prize for which God has called you heavenward in Christ Jesus (see Philippians 3:14). That call is a powerful force, drawing you away from fears that hinder, setting your face toward godly goals, one of which is a renewed, healthy relationship with your child.

Freedom involves genuine communication with your child. God wants you to be able to freely communicate covered-over, denied thoughts and feelings. Perhaps the very idea scares you because you've always been inhibited with this problem child. Maybe He's blasted you with put-downs whenever you've tried to tell him how you feel, even when all you wanted to do was to make peace.

In the previous chapters, you learned how necessary it is to make friends with your own emotions, to allow yourself to experience your own hurt, fear and guilt just as they are, recognizing all along that no matter what has happened, you are forgiven by God. We hope you've begun challenging your misbeliefs, and that you are learning how to tell yourself the truth.

Now we encourage you to consider approaching your child—to begin cultivating vulnerability and openness.

Willing to Be Friends Again

You may hesitate. Why should you have to make the first move? Perhaps you say to yourself, "It was the kid who violated the relationship, so he ought to make the first move to put it back together. Sure I'm willing to be friends—I'm here whenever he wants to come and ask me for forgiveness!"

As a parent, we believe that it's your responsibility to take the initiative in repairing the damage. When you make the first effort, in fact, you are exercising the God-given role of a parent. You take the initiative, make the first move—and hope with all your heart that your child will respond.

You are *willing to be friends* for perhaps the first time in the history of your relationship with a problem child.

As an Equal

All parents must learn, eventually, to treat older children as peers rather than as juveniles. We aren't saying that at a particular age the fourth commandment is set aside. But we expect a thirty-year-old to show honor in a different way than an eleven-year-old. Stop expecting your son or daughter to *do it* because you say to do it, to *think it* because you want them to think it, or to *feel it* because you think it's the right way to feel.

This is no easy task. For years you've been a provider, a protector, and a watchman, knowing full well the dangers in life and what failure brings. If your child is harming himself in one way or another, it's easy to "act like a parent" in the same way you always did, which is to take charge. It's easy to assume that your child agrees that you know best. It's hard to step back and give your child room to grow.

Now some parents seem to come by such wisdom naturally. Others may say, "You don't know *my* kid! There's no way to treat my kid like an adult, or equal. When he starts acting his age, then I'll start treating him like an adult!"

True, it may appear that your child *needs* to be treated like a juvenile. Your child may even have deliberately cultivated in you the belief that he is helpless and immature, so it's vital for you to continue acting as if he is really eight years old. How else can she make you play your accustomed role of facilitator for her impulsive, maladaptive acting-out? How else can he keep you shelling out support money until he finds the job that's just exactly right for him? You probably think you have a right to tell such a child what to do, since it always falls to you to bail him out. The truth is, if you don't treat him as an adult you will *always* be bailing him out. *Is this what you want?*

For one thing, *you* need to stop acting like the guardian of a juvenile. Samuel Butler observed, "Some people seem compelled by unkind fate to parental servitude for life. There is no form of penal servitude much worse than this." Isn't it time you let yourself out of jail?

Even more important, your children need to be allowed to grow up and to be respected as self-determining human beings. As they reach adulthood, they want desperately for you to stop telling them what to do. They want to decide for themselves—to be free to make their own mistakes. You may need to make the commitment to let them bear the responsibility for those mistakes.

Their real need—so deep they may not even be aware of it—is to become aware of their utter helplessness apart from God. If you keep taking the place of God—bailing them out and telling them what to do—they will never discover that they need to throw themselves entirely upon Him. It's true that real self-determination results from God-determination, when a person brings his life under the rule of God.

The "Show-Stopper"

Jeff's father brought the family-therapy session to a halt by barking at his son. "You can't possibly make a living as an actor. And anyway, they're all perverts," Tony began. "You get into that stuff and you'll die of AIDS. Get a regular job, Jeff. What's wrong with a little hard work? Get your lily-white hands dirty for a change. Get a job driving a truck, like I did, and stop imagining you're a movie star. I'm sick of supporting you while you waste your life with a bunch of sick-o's."

Jeff, a twenty-four-year-old, curly-haired guy who made you want to think of him as a boy, looked at Bill and shrugged. It was a gesture as if to say, "See? I told you this is what he'd do."

Jeff's mother, June, just shook her head and shifted her gaze out the window.

The family had sought help because of conflict between Tony and Jeff which, though persisting in one form or another since Jeff was a little boy, had now reached a crisis. Jeff's casual, halfhearted stabs at getting a job galled Tony almost as much as his son's involvement with theater arts and evident lack of interest in dating. Still, he supported Jeff financially and allowed him to live at home, though June had argued with him often that he should let their son take responsibility for his own support. "Why should he get serious about working," argued June, "as long as you continue to give him all the money he needs?" It was as if Tony had determined to keep Jeff where he could give him orders, and thus change Jeff's behavior! This family would eventually reach profound understanding among themselves. They would have to before Jeff and Tony would be able to relate as friends.

But one thing was evident at this very first interview—at least to Bill, and apparently to June as well—there could be no progress until Tony gave up trying to make his son follow orders like a juvenile. He would have to accept his son's right to make choices as an adult. He would have to acknowledge Jeff's right to choose even wrong things—and to face the consequences of wrong choices. Tony would have to stop talking down to Jeff and giving him orders no matter how threatened he felt by his son's behavior.

Tony touched off the next session by yelling, "I can't respect him, the way he's screwing up!" You can probably see that Tony was big on "show-stopper" kinds of lines—designed to "force" the world to see things his way. Unfortunately, they don't work.

While your child may not seem to you to have earned much respect, at the very least you can begin to see him as having value to God. To *earn respect* and to be *given dignity* are separate matters. Honor your child's God-given dignity and watch what happens. To have respect for someone means to *consider him as having worth.*

Quite often, as parents, we relate with our kids on a peer level in some ways—only to fall into the trap of putting them in their place in other ways. It is important to understand your deeper reasons for relapsing into the "controlling parent" mode. What are the misbeliefs underlying your unwillingness to let go? Do you tell yourself that God can't be trusted to handle your child and his needs, so you have to move into the gap left by God's failures?

Put Yourself in Their Shoes

Who is this complex person, your child? What's it like to be at the center of his personality and look out on the world through his eyes? What does life look like from there? What things does he like and dislike? What does he want from you? How would he like to be treated by his parents?

While you're standing, mentally, in your offspring's shoes, ask yourself questions: What is your child going through with his peers, with school, with his job? How does he feel about you? His sister? His brother? Is he depressed, anxious, angry, frustrated? How does he handle stress? Does he run from it, does he run into it? What are his misbeliefs? Why does he feel he must do the things he does, the things that create so much havoc? Try not to jump back into your own shoes too soon. Otherwise your own old thoughts, judgments, and beliefs (possibly *mis*beliefs) will obliterate his perspective. Take a good, long look from your child's perspective.

Perhaps you'll recall the story of Candy and her mother in chapter 6. It was only after Candy's mother began trying to look at the situation from Candy's point of view that she was able to empathize with her daughter's pain, grief, sorrow and guilt. That completely changed the way Candy's mother thought and felt about her daughter. No longer did the thought of Candy automatically call forth anger and resentment. Instead, Mother became aware of a new softness, an empathetic understanding of Candy's frailties, a release from bitterness, and a new acceptance.

Initiate Vulnerability

What if your child is aware of some specific wrong you have done to him? It will be necessary to confess that wrong.

Suppose you have pointedly examined yourself and honestly cannot come up with much to confess. It may be time to ask your child for his perspective. Ask if you've hurt him in ways you're unaware of. Yes, it can hurt to hear your sins recounted from your child's lips. Yes, it might make you shudder even to think of what he may be holding against you. And yes, you might have spent a lifetime dodging such a confrontation. But remember: God's sharpest scalpels cut clean. Keep in mind the goal of freedom.

Here are some confession guidelines:

Confess only if you are truly guilty. Some people are too anxious to confess to things they haven't actually done, or to things that are so vague and nit-picking they're actually confessing to nothing. Don't go through the motions unless you have real sins to confess.

Second, confess only if your confession serves a purpose and will bring healing to your relationship with your older child. Some people confess "sins" that can only hurt the other person. It won't bring healing to say, "I have never loved you as much as I loved your sister, because she was pretty and you were the ugly duckling." This is not a confession; it's a heartless attack.

Confess *your* failings, not your child's. It's not a confession but an accusation to say, "Well, I guess I did put you down in front of your friends a lot—but you never considered my feelings or cared how much you hurt me, did you?"

Notice the word "but" in that last sentence. If you find yourself planning a confession with a "but" in it, you'd better examine it carefully. It's probably a self-serving defensive accusation and not a confession at all. There will be time to deal with your older child's faults later on.

Those Three Little Words: "I Love You"

Sometimes we can best communicate human love by saying, "I love you." But there are other loving ways to cross the gap between you and your child.

Almost everyone wants to be loved, but each of us has different preferences as to *how* love is packaged. How has your child liked to be loved over the years? Has she longed to cuddle close to you, sighing contentedly with the relief of acceptance? Or has he preferred the kind of love that comes through giving respectful distance? Does she hate being fussed over? Does he want you to give him space?

From the time she was an infant, our granddaughter Jenny has enjoyed snuggling. She manages to crawl so deeply into your arms that every part of her body is held or caressed as she looks into your eyes, saying silently, I love you too!

Our little grandson is quite a contrast. Jakey, Jenny's little brother, wants his space. Occasionally, Jake wants to cuddle, but only briefly. Soon he wriggles away, usually preferring to hear loving words or praise for good behavior. Partly because, at age two, there is very little that he does to warrant praise, it's much more difficult to show him love than his compliant, cuddly sister!

And there are times when Jake doesn't want to hear you talk.

One day when we took Jakey to the park, he sat stoically

in the swing, pensive, as we chattered on. Soon, head bent down in total concentration, he said, "Don't talk to me!" He wanted at that moment to be left alone. (We have enjoyed using this phrase with one another ever since as a signal that we want our own space.) When we mentioned going to get a treat, Jake quickly rejoined our company. Animated, involved, he began chattering like a chipmunk about the virtues of popcorn. Evidently, his channel for love at that point happened to be popcorn!

Be assured that even after your child has matured, he wants to know you love and value him. Whether it's a hand on the shoulder, a hug, a kiss, a fishing trip, or a ball game, you can establish a special way to communicate acceptance and love. Find what is pleasing and reinforcing, even if it isn't what you'd prefer.

One Way to Say, "I Love You"

The hour had grown late. Candy and her father talked in low voices outside a motel room in Carmel Valley, California. As the midnight fog swirled around them, father and daughter opened their hearts to each other with a life-changing intimacy that had never before seemed possible.

Candy's father was painfully aware of the trip to Hawaii looming ahead for his daughter. It was a return to the scene of heartbreak, for it was in Hawaii that Candy's pregnancy had occurred so many years ago, and it was there that the terrible decision was made to abort the baby. To Candy, Hawaii meant guilt, shame and anguish. As they talked, her old distress surfaced in tears.

Dad knew what the tears meant. And he knew he had to re-open an old wound in order to help the healing. "Honey," he murmured softly, "we've never talked about this, because it's hard to do. But I think it's time I shared your pain. How do you feel about seeing Hawaii again?"

To Candy, this invitation to share her feelings was the expression of love for which she'd waited a long time. Their relationship over the years had been fine—on the surface. By unspoken agreement pain was never discussed.

"You're right, Daddy," she replied. "I want to talk, even though it's not easy. It would be easier to forget the past and move on. But I've tried that and it hasn't worked. I have to go back to Hawaii and confront the place of pain. I want to face the past and—with Jesus' help, and Bill's help—deal with it once and for all."

"I know it was my fault in the first place," her dad offered. "If it hadn't been for my own failures—if your mom and I hadn't destroyed your home—you would never have gotten pregnant. There would have been no abortion. I'm so sorry for the pain I've brought to you, honey. Can you ever forgive me?" Tears were now welling up in his eyes, too.

Candy's heart was melting. "Daddy, I do forgive you for your sins against me. But I'm responsible for my own actions. I've been pretty sinful all by myself. I was wrong, and it's no one else's fault. I'm so sorry for hurting and disappointing you."

Now he gently drew her close. Stroking her hair, he whispered, "You were made in *my* image, just as we were all made in God's image. When you hurt, I hurt."

Candy couldn't believe what she was hearing. Could this conversation really be happening after so many years of avoidance and covering up? There was more.

Her father encouraged her to face the pain, to believe that the Lord Jesus has forgiven all of her sins as well as all of his. Then he encouraged her to close the door to the past and to move on to a new life. Assuming his proper role as spiritual leader in the family, even this late in life, he instructed his thirty-nine-year-old daughter to walk in the grace and love of her heavenly Father.

Candy's heart soared! Her father's tenderness and honesty washed away the residue left by years of bitterness, agony and frustration. What her father gave her was this: He loved her in the particular way Candy needed to be loved by him at that moment.

Perhaps you need to open up long-closed wounds. Perhaps that is one way your problem child wants to be loved by you right now.

Prepare for Uncertainties

Who knows how your child will react to your new openness? Perhaps you think it will be difficult, and you may be right. So prepare for uncertainties. You're trying something new. Remember, you used to

- have shouting matches ... now you're remaining calm;
- hurl insults at each other ... now you're treating him with dignity;
- defend yourself ... now you can confess your faults without offering any rationale or defense;
- walk away shaking your head at her hard-headed stubbornness ... now you can stay with her patiently and lovingly, trying to get a new message across;
- feel weak and helpless or frustrated in his presence ... now you are strengthened by God;
- keep away from her emotionally ... now you're opening up, ready to face the hard stuff with her, knowing that it's okay and even a relief to finally walk through emotions together;
- feel at a loss to know how to proceed ... now you're learning new skills and have, in prayer, deepened your trust that God is with you.

Yes, it may be hard for you and for your child. When you have spent twenty years (more or less) doing things a certain way, and then suddenly change, even a change for the better can be overwhelming. Your son or daughter may not like the changes in you. This might mean that, because you've changed, he'll have to change, too. The following are among the most likely responses you might encounter.

Denial. Let's keep pretending that we don't need to be honest. Besides, to admit you've been hurt means that you may be hurt more deeply.

Anger, and outright refusal to forgive. Maybe in words or actions your child may say, "*You* can change if you want to, but don't expect it of me. It's too late. You blew it. I'm not about to soften up or change, so forget it."

Emotionlessness. Perhaps, like the old you, your child will be unable to get in touch with her own feelings. Gripped by fear, she won't let herself feel. This is a protection against further injury.

Real change! Of course, it's possible that your child will be ready, even if a little scared, to accept your efforts to work out an open relationship. It may be that his heart will melt, and that you will discover him to be as desirous as you for a wonderful new friendship.

Earning Trust

Many people believe that the trust of friends and loved ones is a right guaranteed at birth. This is a false assumption. Trust has to be earned. It is not your God-given duty to place infinite trust in your child. Love, yes; trust, no.

By the same token, there is no particular reason for your child to trust *you* without your having earned that trust. If trust has been ruptured by some failing of yours, you must earn trust by changed behavior.

You begin to do this by making amends where possible. It isn't always possible to set right what's been done wrong, but sometimes it is possible. If you have deceived your child, you can tell him the truth. If you have withheld deserved approval, you can offer heartfelt positive reinforcement now.

Be careful not to overcompensate. In your eagerness to make up to your child for real failings, don't make the mistake of showering him with more than is due. The guilt-ridden parents who pay rent on their adult child's apartment, or furnish a new car every two years, or hand out cash on request are not making restitution—they're making "guilt payments." In a word: Don't.

Most of all, allow time for God to work your words into the heart of your child. Remember how long it has taken you to get to this point. Be patient.

Take a Deep Breath

Continue to tell yourself the truth about God: He is your confidence, your strength, your all-sufficient supply. In all probability, you'll fail a time or two as you try new ways of relating to your child. When this happens, turn immediately to your Source. Tell yourself: "[I am] confident of this very thing: He who began a good work in [me] will perfect it until the day of Jesus Christ" (Philippians 1:6). Our responsibility is to trust God. The responsibility for results belongs to Him.

From what do you need to be liberated in your relationship with your son or daughter? (See John 8:32, 33.)

9

Freeing Your Child

Children seem to be born with the spirit of Patrick Henry. "Give me liberty, or give me death!" is their motto. It rarely occurs to them that liberty means responsibility.

Can you recall how vital it seemed, when you were a young adult, to stand on your own? Death would be better than to be tied to your mom's apron strings! In the same way, your sons and daughters want to be free to do whatever they please. It just so happens, however, that they also want the convenience of using your resources when the need arises. It doesn't occur to some grown children that their parents, too, have freedom and no longer owe them everything.

Striking a Blow for Freedom

In an earlier chapter, we introduced Roger and Teresa and their problem child, Stephanie.

At twenty-four, Stephanie planned to live in her parents home, at least for the indefinite future. Life was made comfortable by Teresa's hot meals, the warmth of the family circle, and having the use of her parents' cars when her junker quit. Especially convenient was the baby-care service. Living with her folks, she could entrust her two children to their care, and she could come and go at will. If another out-of-wedlock baby came, Mother and Dad would be there to love and care for it just as they'd accepted the other two. Sure, they'd gotten upset when she had announced each pregnancy—but they got over it. Then they'd enfold Stephanie and her babies into their loving embrace. Stephanie never imagined her parents would call a halt to her freeloading.

In counselling, Roger and Teresa had finally faced the truth. They'd been fostering Stephanie's irresponsible dependency by seldom letting her bear the consequences of her actions. They had assumed, as many parents do, that they owed her whatever she wanted from them. They thought about their innocent little grandchildren, and wanted desperately to shield them from the selfishness of their mother.

But they saw that there was no way to ultimately shield Stephanie from all the difficulties she created. She would always make more trouble for herself than they could rescue her from. And they couldn't save their grandchildren from her willfulness, no matter how hard they tried. Stephanie and the babies were in God's hands. They talked with each other, prayed for guidance, and decided that they would now have to love their daughter in a very different way.

When Roger and Teresa finally confronted her, their unprecedented calm and self-control threw Stephanie off-balance. Never before had they refused to be misused by her! Previously, she'd simply threatened to keep them from seeing their grandchildren ever again, and they'd backed down. But this time it didn't work.

When Roger and Teresa quietly told Stephanie it was time to move out on her own, she became hysterical.

When the screaming stopped, they went on. They told her that they objected to her sexual promiscuity. They didn't bombard her with Bible passages—Stephanie had learned them long ago. They simply told her they believed her behavior was wrong and injurious to herself, to them, and most of all to her babies, and that they were no longer going to support it. They told her the truth in gentleness and kindness.

Not only that, they informed Stephanie of their expectations for her:

She was to move to an apartment of her own; she would be responsible for her own expenses and those of the children; visits with the children would be at their discretion, and not whenever Stephanie wanted to "unload" them. To make sure that she understood the seriousness of their decision, they were changing all locks on the house.

Lastly, they assured her they had no intention of nagging her about her behavior. They would not initiate a discussion about her lifestyle again. If she wanted to live on welfare the rest of her life, that was her decision. If she wanted to get a reputable job, or go to school, that would also be her decision. She was free to make what she wanted of her own life—and to live with the consequences. They assured her of their love, and reminded her that they would always love her children too.

They had placed their child in God's hands.

Stephanie

Stephanie considered all of this "outrageous." What nonsense was this? What about her *rights*? They couldn't lock her out of her own house, could they? She ranted and raved.

For the first time ever, they didn't back down.

Stephanie gradually got the idea that they meant what they said. After a time, she cooled down. It dawned on her that she would be the loser if she snapped the cord of love that bound her parents to her. She agreed to accept their terms.

After simmering down further, Stephanie even found she could enjoy being an adult with her parents. Grudgingly at first, she felt herself respecting them for their resoluteness. She also admitted that being on her own had its good side, though she was uncomfortable thinking of herself as a "welfare mother." But she *was* actually surviving without her parents' help.

The four steps that Roger and Teresa took have worked

for others. If you have an older child who has used your love while irresponsibly pursuing his own agenda, telling you his choices are none of your business (except that you have to *pay* for them!), then you might want to use this family as a model. Maybe it's time to decide that you're going to stop facilitating rebellious and destructive behavior.

Isn't it time for you to do your child a favor, telling him you believe he's wrong and that his actions are troubling to you? Your child is so valuable to God and to you that it's time you called a halt to the part you play in making rebellion easy. You might want to say calmly:

> I love you very much, so I'm going to make some things clear to you. In case I haven't told you straight out, I don't like what you're doing in _____ . I want you to know that because I love you. Furthermore, I will expect you to _____ from this point on, so that it will be clear that I'm not making your behavior easier for you. I intend to carry this out by doing the following things: _____ . I want you to know, too, that I don't intend to harp on these things, just to carry them out as I have described them.

The Great Temptation

This temptation will come like a thief in the night: You'll hear the voice within telling you that your new stance of firmness and honesty is a huge mistake.

Don't think you're going to come through this without a war in your mind! Prepare for it. Fortify yourself with the truth. Power up with the Word of God. Again and again, God's Word asserts that parental love is robust and strong, not wimpy.

Correcting Eli for failing to take a firm hand against his sons' abuses of priestly authority, God asked him, "Why do you honor your sons above me?" (1 Samuel 2:29). Here are other passages encouraging parents to stand strong in dealing with their children:

Proverbs 22:15
Proverbs 19:15
Ephesians 6:4
Hebrews 12:5

"I'd Better Bail Him Out!"

"But shouldn't we help our children when they're struggling to succeed?" Eva was near tears—and *angry*.

What *she* meant about helping children to succeed was not what you might think, however. She was referring to her frantic desire to rescue her son, Peter, who'd been picked up again for running cocaine.

"He's not a criminal. He's really such a good boy," she insisted. "He's promised me he'll stop using drugs and dealing if only I'll get him a lawyer and save him from jail just one more time." She thought it was possible that someone had planted those drugs on Peter. He'd had so many bad breaks! Most of his teachers had it in for him all through his school years. Now she was convinced she ought to bail Peter out again.

Take a moment to go through this "habitual rescuers" inventory. Have you

- . . . habitually canceled all your plans to do whatever your older child claimed he needed you to do?
- . . . agreed to let her come to live with you, when she can furnish her own living quarters and you don't really want her in yours?
- . . ."loaned" him money over and over again, never to be repaid?
- . . . felt a compulsion to make life easy for her so she won't have to struggle?
- . . . felt duty-bound to trust him, in spite of his untrustworthy record?
- . . . tried to help her avoid punishment when you *knew* she was guilty?

Have you ever considered *why* you want to run to the rescue, and why you repeatedly move heaven and earth to bail out this kid? We'd like to offer some possible explanations.

For one thing, you love your child, and you're willing to do anything to help him make it. But help has limits. If you can't see that there comes a point where all that you're doing no longer helps but hinders, then your love will become harmful.

Another reason is *embarrassment*. What will people think? Your relatives may very well have decided long ago that you're doing everything wrong or your child wouldn't have such problems. Your friends may be muttering about how you're "ruining" your child. And now, if he doesn't succeed, they'll all know for sure you're the worst parent who ever lived. Having others judge and condemn us can be a very powerful threat.

Yet another reason we come to the rescue is that we want our children to love and approve of us. We want to receive the reward of their acceptance and approval. Very often, for whatever reason, problem children develop the knack of keeping us hungry for their positive feedback. They've learned that we try harder that way.

Sometimes we rescue without even thinking. It's close to instinctive for us to run to the rescue when a child is in danger. And sometimes we fail to change that instinctive behavior when the child has grown up. The honest fact is that some of our actions are no longer appropriate.

Consequences

Kevin's parents warned him not to hang around with Jim, the neighborhood daredevil. Jim had a record of trouble. Besides owning a deck of speeding tickets, he'd collected a couple of DWI's, and would lose his license the next time. Sad to say, next time wasn't soon enough.

One July evening, Jim and Kevin went out to "cruise." They bought a twelve-pack of beer, Jim cranked the stereo to full volume and floored the accelerator.

When the police arrived at the scene of their head-on collision with an oak tree, they knew it would be a miracle to find anyone alive. Improbably, both men survived the crash! Kevin was in far worse shape than Jim, and spent two months in the hospital recovering from broken bones and undergoing numerous surgical procedures.

Kevin learned the consequences of ignoring his parents' warnings. He paid dearly for his irresponsibility, in more ways than one. In addition to his pain, Kevin was not covered by his parents' hospitalization insurance. He will be making payments on his medical bills for years. Though they were tempted to bail him out, his parents resolutely resisted. Many times, with tears rolling down his gaunt cheeks, Kevin berated himself for not listening. Painful consequences, yes. But through them Kevin was able to learn a number of valuable lessons. He repented and his life has changed. He's set out to achieve goals. Who knows? If Mom and Dad had picked up the tab, Kevin might still be courting injuries and death instead of the young woman who will soon be his bride.

A Golden Rule of Parenting

Children are different. Each parent-child relationship is a special case and presents its own peculiar challenges. Perhaps your children haven't quite left adolescence and haven't quite made it to adulthood, so he's still living in your home and still your responsibility. Perhaps she's mentally or physically handicapped and will always need your help and support.

If there are concrete reasons why you can't reasonably expect your child to move to full independence and autonomy now, you can still apply one "golden rule" of parenting:

Let every child
do what he can
for himself.

If *he* can do it, don't do it for him! So you can think of a million reasons for bailing him out and doing things *for* him. None of those reasons are good enough to deprive your child of the chance to mature and to stand on his own two feet. Let him learn dignity and self-respect by *doing*, even if you have to risk that he'll do it wrong.

It's excruciating to see your child make mistakes. But it's exhilarating to see him succeed.

When your child makes a bad choice, or acts irresponsible, continue to reinforce your determination with truths like these:

- Few mistakes are truly catastrophic—and this one probably isn't a major disaster either.
- I've done the best I could to train him. If my performance isn't perfect, what do I expect of another limited, sinful human being?
- God is at work in my child, and the completion of His work may take a while.

And remember *always*: Your child is in the hands of his heavenly Father. Can you think of a better place for him?

List some things your child can do for himself that you are presently doing for him. See how God wants His children to be free and to grow up, by looking up and studying the following passages: Ephesians 4:15; 1 Peter 2:2; 2 Peter 3:18.

10

Tuning In

How often have you bellowed at your child, "LISTEN TO ME!!" Much more often, perhaps, than you've said the words, "I want to understand what you're feeling and thinking."

How often have you tuned out a complaint or problem, thinking, *I already know what's coming.* So instead of listening, you interrupt with a "solution."

How often have you told yourself, "They never listen to a word I say." All your "discussions" with this problem child dissolve into arguments.

The One Model Parent

One of the most beautiful things we can understand about our heavenly Father is that He is a great God of self-revelation. He wants to be known by us. To that end, He has spoken to us by His Word. He says what He means and means what He says.

Isn't this a great model for us as earthly parents? Too often, our "conversations" involve only orders and instructions, lectures, preachments, and correction. Why are we so afraid to know and be known?

God also *hears* what His children have to say. The Bible

describes Him as inclining His ear toward us, His children. The God and Father of all listens to *you* when you speak.

Perhaps you've never considered how little you may really know your child. Let's take a closer look at this crucial need.

When the Problem Is *Not* Listening

Many parents who feel they can't relate to their adult child ache over the fractured relationship. Part of the ache is that they sincerely believe they've done all they could to mend it, but their best shot wasn't good enough.

In every single instance of those parents we've counseled, the problem was *not* that they hadn't tried. The root of the difficulty was not a failure to *tell things* to their alienated child. It was a failure to *hear* what was said to them. As a result, their son or daughter erected walls. And thereafter, all advice and assorted "shoulds" had fallen on deaf ears.

Do you hear yourself in any of the following?

- You should go to church every Sunday. Didn't we raise you to love the house of the Lord?
- Your lifestyle is *not* what we taught you at all—it's awful. You need to stop what you're doing. Period.
- Sure, I might have made some mistakes, and if I have I'm sorry. But *you* . . .
- You should get a job. You'd feel a lot better if you did.
- You didn't come over last weekend, and your mother felt just terrible. You should get over here to see her, you know.

Telling vs. Listening

We've met with many parents who made frequent "suggestions" like those above. They were irritated that the responses of their children were so troubling. "He just won't listen." "She says it's her business, and I should stay out of it." "I get no response. *Nothing.*" These folks cannot see that such replies indicate they've made one simple but major mistake: Like most of us, they concentrated more on *telling* than on *listening*. The results were dismal because their children sensed they were not being heard. When kids who have parents like this talk to *their* therapists, they say things like, "My mom can't understand me at all." "My dad gets upset if I try to explain to him how I feel." "My parents want to run my life like they did when I was ten. They don't care what I think. They don't even *know* what I think."

The Transforming Secret

Do you merely want to change your child? Or do you want to transform your relationship?

Those who do not care to learn about relationships have no interest in listening. They want to be *listened to*. They want their kids to *do* what they want. They want to run their kids' lives. They may even want to feel important and respected by throwing their weight around. But the secret of good adult relationships is listening.

Perhaps it's time you sorted out your relationship goals with your child. You have them whether or not you realize it.

Take a little time to honestly explore these questions:

Do you want your child to change? Very likely you do. If your son has announced his preference for a homosexual lifestyle, you want him to change. If your daughter has been promiscuous, you want her to stop. If your child is a perpetual student who has squeezed every vestige of religious upbringing out of her life in favor of humanism, you want her to return to her faith. If your child's therapy has taught him to blame you, you want him to take responsibility for his life. Of course you want change. This, however, is only one of several goals, and it's important to clarify and focus on others, as well.

Do you want to MAKE your child spiritually healthy? Do you try to talk her into doing what's good for her? Some parents have trouble realizing that they cannot make their older children be or do anything. Regaining spiritual wholeness might require operations and events over which a parent has absolutely no control. Tell yourself the truth: Your child's spiritual well-being may be harmed by your demands for change. Instead, try making your point once—and then learn to listen, allowing the Holy Spirit to work at His own pace.

Do you want your child to listen to you? You may want this so much that you believe his eternal well-being depends on your words. As a result, you become louder and more aggressive as you try to hammer home your point. When you think you're not being heard you bear down. Intensify. Sure you want to be heard—but do you want it badly enough to ruin the relationship?

Or do you want a good relationship with your child? Open lines? Relatively warm and positive communications? Frequent contact? Do you prefer this to an atmosphere of tension, anger and frustration?

Once you've determined your goals, consider their order of priority. Otherwise you'll try to achieve all of them at once, and some of them may be contradictory at a given time. In other words, you may have to put up with some anger in order to have an open relationship. You may have to accept as a fact that your child does things that are blatantly wrong if you're going to get near enough to him to love him. You may have to tolerate some very unpleasant reality if you are to enter into deep, close and meaningful communication.

How to Really Hear Your Child

Here are some habits that can cause a parent to become "hearing impaired." These are practices you will want to work on if you find them in yourself:

Defensiveness: "Well, maybe I *did* try too hard to help you choose friends with good character. But you have a lot of nerve telling me I never approved of your choice of friends. Where do you get off . . ."

Musing about yourself, your reactions, your agreement, or

disagreement: "I'm not sure *I'd* make that choice. When I was a kid . . ."

Tuning out mentally to form your own rebuttal: "I'll tell him—if he ever shuts up—how I learned to handle this problem. (Where does he come up with these senseless, half-baked solutions anyway?)"

Formulating judgments and evaluations while your son or daughter is trying to be heard: "Where did she get that stupid idea? Probably from some of this women's lib philosophy they're pushing at school. I've got to let her know how inane this is."

Acting like the sage, or the heroic deliverer: "*I* can show you how to resolve this. We'll get it all fixed."

Acting like an interrogator: "You still haven't made sense to me. Tell me—why on earth did you. . . ?"

"Itching" for a chance to point out faults: "There! You've just said it yourself. Your boss 'bugs' you. That's your whole problem—your attitude."

Eliminating the six bad habits listed above will carry you a long way toward improving the quality of hearing.

The next time you are "conversing" with your child, why not pay attention to your own performance as a hearer? How would you grade yourself? Tune in to your own behavior. What do you do and think, how do you respond when your child wants to talk—or when he wants to be silent and say nothing at all?

If you come to the conclusion that you spend a lot of time judging, waiting to talk, looking for faults, planning your own next speeches, set yourself the goal of eliminating your faulty hearing behaviors. Get to work replacing them with energetic relationship-advancing listening behavior.

You'll be surprised at what you learn about the inner workings of your own child.

Look up James 1:19. Think about a conversation where you feel another person *was* listening to you. List the things he did that made you feel that way.

11

Hope

We all have days when we want to pull the covers up over our head, and shut out the world. But when you can foresee nothing but tragedy for your child, you wonder if life will ever be normal again. Perhaps you're almost ready to call it quits. Perhaps deep inside, you've entertained the thought that God hasn't come through for you. So why keep praying? Why try to stick this thing out as a Christian?

"Today, If You Hear His Voice . . ."

Paul, who went through numerous disappointments himself, tells us, "See to it, brothers, that none of you has a sinful, unbelieving heart that turns away from the living God. But *encourage one another daily* . . . so that none of you may be hardened by sin's deceitfulness. . . . Today, if you hear his voice, do not harden your hearts as you did in the rebellion" (Hebrews 3:12, emphasis added).

Even the strongest among us can entertain devilish suggestions that we give up on God. But have you ever noticed how just a few words from the Bible can dispel darkness? It is very important to look closely at what the letter to the Hebrews says to us as grieving parents:

129

- When we choose unbelief, we become deceived and harden our own hearts.
- An unbelieving heart turns away from the living God.
- God has provided encouragement for us. We can hear and obey His voice.
- In our trials, we're sharing in Christ's suffering, so we aren't alone.
- We can hold on firmly, maintaining the same confidence we had when we first came to Christ.
- The Lord has made all this possible by giving us His Word.
- Being encouraged one time will not be enough. We must actively surround ourselves with ongoing encouragement to hang on to the truth. None of us can stand alone.

Encouragement With the Truth

There is nothing like it—the truth that breaks through, like sunshine, bringing light, health, wholeness and peace. The purest fountain of truth lies in the Holy Scriptures because they are uniquely God's Word, and God cannot lie or deny himself. Drench yourself in them, allow God to reveal to you His hope and faithfulness to counter your dismay and discouragement!

There is also a truth that comes as you spend time in honest fellowship with brothers and sisters in the body of Christ. Though you may be tempted to run away sometimes, stop yourself! Instead, surround yourself with good people who can share in the truth with you. Just being around others who know the Word of God helps to ease the distress; and in strong, godly, supportive fellowship, your mind will be better fortified against deception and the hopelessness it brings. Of course, there will be times when you'll be alone with your own thoughts, both good and bad, true and false. These times are necessary. By them, the Lord works growth and maturity. Don't resist them—but don't wallow in isolation either. Spend time with others on a regular basis.

There are also other ways to find the emotional support you need. According to research psychologists Merton and Irene Strommen,[1] there are over 40,000 national self-help organizations in the United States. People are helping people all over the nation to bear up and overcome such problems as alcoholism, drug addiction and abuse, to name a few. We *need* one another, because we can gain new insight into the truth and draw strength from one another as we share.

We encourage you to find a group offering support for those in similar situations to yours. Take some time to check it out. Is it a strong group, and one that will be helpful to you? The marks of a good support group are honesty and truth, combined with love and encouragement. Find a group that will not just tell you you're right all the time, but will occasionally challenge your thinking and your actions. A good support group will tell you when your thinking is wrong. The love other group members offer can be a real life-saver.

If you decide to join a support group, it's imperative to locate one that's healthy and mature. Unfortunately, some groups are composed of people who don't know God's truth themselves and, in addition, have very little common sense. Such groups can hurt more than they help. Sometimes groups become so inbred, dwelling on hurts, that well-meaning people only feed on one another's weakness. Often groups are led by professionals—psychologists, counselors, teachers, clergy—who have been trained to facilitate support groups. But professional direction isn't necessary for a good support group. Truth, love, maturity and wisdom *are* necessary, though, and ought to be manifested.

Smiling Dogs

While the support of a group can be an important source of hope, it isn't the only way we can be lifted up. Learn to value support you find daily, in common occurrences. You

[1]Merton P. Strommen and Irene A. Strommen, *Five Cries of Parents* (San Francisco: Harper and Row, 1985).

can get a lift, for instance, from the warm smile of a check-out lady in your local grocery store, or from the friendly greeting of a neighbor or co-worker. It can even come from a smiling dog.

Each day we are greeted by Mocha, our one hundred pound German Shepherd. A broad smile wraps around her black muzzle, pink tongue hanging out from between large, sharp white spikes you know could shred you. She says, "I love you with all my being" as clearly as her deep brown eyes can communicate, wiggles her massive frame toward us, her tail wagging, thumping and knocking to the floor whatever might be caught in its sweep. She's excited to see us every time we meet her, no matter how often, and tells us by gnawing on one of our hands, massaging it with doggy kisses and slobber, as she takes the hand in her mouth and leads its owner around the house. She loves us unconditionally, or so it seems. When we are hurting Mocha seems to have an uncanny sense that all is not right. She comes to us, offering sympathy in the form of a huge head resting on our laps, or of wanting to hold hands/paws with us. This smiling dog has brought us more comfort than money could ever buy. What a marvelous provision of God!

Whether it's a smiling dog, a cuddly cat, or your pet goldfish, you, too, can be lifted up by God's creation. Evidence suggests that a pet can do you good. If you don't have one, you might like to consider what the love you give to an animal can offer back to you.

Just look around you, and allow the Lord to reveal His love and compassion to you as He offers support in unusual ways.

What You *Don't* Need

Clara felt bad about her two boys. Their sullen hostility and aimless pursuits nearly drove her crazy, so she said. Maybe it was because Ted and Ned were twins that she had double trouble. To "help" herself Clara surrounded herself with maudlin sympathy. Her friends smothered her with romantic ideas of what she "really deserved," fussing about how awful her life was. This is not what Clara needed, but it's what she trained her friends to feed back to her when she was feeling bad.

Occasionally, someone in Clara's church would gently try to offer another side to the truth about pain—its benefits in leading to maturity, and that there is more to life than wallowing in tears. But any attempt to strengthen her went unheard, and Clara alienated the friends who offered her the most hope and freedom. She preferred to remain in a state of weak emotionalism.

While a sympathetic and understanding heart is usually a welcome relief, maudlin sympathy can further ruin a broken heart. You don't need

- an excuse to act bad, using your problem child as justification;
- alcohol, tranquilizers, or staying in bed all day to avoid the reality of life's difficulties;
- the problem to end immediately in order for the devastating pain of it to go away.

Instead, you need the creative work of God to remake your heart and mind.

Recreation

Most of us feel a bit guilty for going out to have a little fun when we're hurting so much. For one thing, we think we won't really enjoy it when things are so bad. For another, we tell ourselves we don't deserve it. Yet one of the most beneficial things we can do is play. We all need the wholesome benefits of recreation. This, too, is God's provision.

When we allow ourselves to relax and have fun, perspective changes. We realize that life does go on, and that we can still be a part of that life. We gain a healthier outlook as we reckon that our problem isn't the only thing happening in the world. It is, in fact, horrible to stay stuck in such a morass, denying God the right to lift our spirits out of despair. Not only is He the God of inward rest, He is the Creator of play and relaxation.

So, find a manner of recreation that suits you. Take your dog for a walk. Play a game of tennis. See a movie. Take a grandchild to the park. Read a good novel. Try square dancing, or a night at the opera. Do what is pleasing and fun for a change. *Give yourself a break: It's okay!*

And as you refresh yourself at leisure, be aware that all you're learning about fun, encouragement and support will one day be useful in ministry to someone else. With all of the pain, fear and guilt you've endured, you'll have opportunity to pass on strength and hope to another who thinks the world has come to an end.

All of these efforts on your own behalf—finding encouragement in the truth, strength in a support group, and refreshment in leisure—will free you up to receive the good life that God wants to give you. And one day, as you have freely received, you will be able to give. (See Matthew 10:8.)

In this way, you are a minister of the gospel of hope in the making!

Look up the following passages. What is the gift of God for each one? Hebrews 3:13; Psalm 42:11; Psalm 43:3; Psalm 36:7.

12

The Invitation to Rest

Perhaps these words will seem impossible to you at first glance: God has a resting place for you, right in the middle of your family struggles. This rest can become more real than strife, hurt, fear, or guilt.

Rest is a promise of God, and His Word is trustworthy. Unlike the promises of men, God's Word offers restoration, strength and hope.

You may be saying, "I'm ready! How do I get to this resting place?"

The first step is simple. Jesus invites us, saying, "Come unto me all who are weary and burdened, and *I* will give you rest. Take my yoke upon you and learn from me, for I am gentle and humble in heart, and you will find rest for your souls. For my yoke is easy and my burden is light" (Matthew 11:28, 29).

Something significant happens when we commit ourselves to the Lord day by day, "yoking" ourselves to Him. No longer can we go our own proud, independent way. Instead, we find that we *and* our burdens are linked to Another. He alone is able to help carry the load. When we begin to depend in every way upon Him, we realize that He never expected us to shoulder the task by ourselves. He wanted to be intimately involved all along. So our proud, independent self-effort can finally cease as we return to the Lord in humility.

The Way to Rest

Hebrews describes the rest God provides for His people. This rest we enter by *obedience* and *faith*. Like the early people of Israel, we can choose to wander around in the desert for forty years—we can spend our days grumbling and complaining, hardening our hearts against God, insisting that He isn't doing things right. We can, in essence, create a rift with Him. Or we can put our trust in the only One who is able to save us and, ultimately, turn all things to good.[1]

It's important for you to see that you will not enter this wonderful "rest" in this lifetime if you have not confronted basic unbelief about God—a problem that is common to most people. What are the *un*beliefs we, as parents, can harbor, keeping us unsettled and inwardly weary all the time?

Unbelief

Entering God's rest is impossible if we harbor unbelief—telling ourselves that God won't do what He promises, or that He doesn't care. When we allow ourselves these notions, we make God out to be a liar, since He has repeatedly told us of His love and of His desire to answer our prayers.

Second, it's easy to harbor the misbelief that God is not really capable of handling our child's problems. The issue rests on whether you're willing to believe what God says of himself, for He has declared over and over in His Word that He is able to save. To rebellious Israel, God had the prophet Isaiah proclaim: "In repentance and rest you shall be saved, in quietness and trust is your strength. But you were not willing!" Why were they not willing? Because they con-

---

[1]If you would like to read more about healing the rift with God, see *The Hidden Rift With God,* by William Backus (Minneapolis: Bethany House Publishers, 1990).

cluded that God's promise could not be counted on. So they missed the strength they could have had through trust.

To you and to me, He says, "Come—trust Me, and enter into my rest!"

Relinquishment

Learning to rest requires that we come to the end of our rope. This means that we lift the restrictions off God. That we stop telling Him what He can do, must do, had *better* do for our children.

In her book, *Beyond Ourselves*, Catherine Marshall teaches one of the most valuable lessons a Christian can learn. Her life turned upside-down when her husband died, and she was left to raise their nine-year-old-son, Peter, on her own. How did she do it? "My life," she said, "became a continuous exercise in the art of relinquishing *all* the burdens to God. And in exchange, He gave me rest."

You may be wondering, "How do I relinquish my burden to God? How can I just stay put, and not run off to join the battle? How do we stay in that place of rest, maintaining complete confidence in Him?"

The answer: By getting our own self-talk lined up with God's Word about himself. When we hear ourselves questioning whether God can really be trusted with our child, it's important to challenge such notions, again and again if necessary. Thus we use what Wordsworth once called "wise passiveness." It is always wisdom to trust God.

Wisdom vs. Instinct

As a normal parent, you have instincts that motivate you to love, to comfort, and even to fight and die for your child if necessary. Such deep impulses go beyond intellect, beyond judgment, and even beyond will.

The instincts appropriate when your child was a baby led you to do most everything for him. For a time, his well-being was your full-time job. His total dependence on you made that appropriate! But what now?

Sometimes, parents' instinctive impulse to treat a son or daughter like a helpless child endures past its usefulness. Now that the season of total dependence is over, it's important to act with more wisdom and less instinct. Wisdom learns from experience and adapts to change, seeking godly understanding of the current situation. God's wisdom knows no end. "By wisdom God founded the earth; by understanding, he established the heavens; by his knowledge the deeps were broken up, and the skies drip with dew," says Proverbs 3:19.

The wisdom we receive from God is more powerful than instinct, because it can adapt to new situations and guide us through unusual difficulties. True wisdom grows out of such a close relationship with God and such an attentive heeding of His Word that we begin, in a tiny measure, to think as God thinks and to understand as He does. We can trust Him to supply us with wisdom if we ask. (See James 1:5.) We can return to Him over and over again for wisdom to replace outmoded instinct. And so it is wisdom that helps us remain in His promised rest.

Let's look at several examples to see how this works:

- *Instinct says:* Stay alert. Don't let the problem escape your attention for a moment. *Wisdom says:* Rest in God. Let Him give the situation His constant care and attention.
- *Instinct says:* Stay in control or everything will go wrong. *Wisdom says:* I will give God control and trust Him to take care of my child.
- *Instinct says:* It's up to me to make things right, because I probably made them wrong to begin with. *Wisdom says:* It's up to the Lord. I will hide in the shadow of His wings. I will relinquish my child and his problems to the Lord.
- *Instinct says:* I must win my child's approval. *Wisdom says:* My child's approval is desirable but not essential. God's approval is vital for me.
- *Instinct says:* He's my baby. I just have to do it for him. *Wisdom says:* He's an adult, or close to it. I love him,

but he's on his own—and responsible to God now.

- *Instinct says:* You must not rest! *Wisdom invites:* Enter into the rest of God.

Wait for the Alarm

When our four kids became teenagers, our inner sense of "rest" was rattled as never before! The most challenging situation for us was when one of them was out for the evening. How would we know for certain when that child was safely home in bed? We'd try to stay awake, lying in bed until we heard the front door close. But we worried. What if we fell asleep?

Bill devised a brilliant scheme. We set an alarm clock to go off an hour after curfew time. We put the clock in our bedroom, but ran a cord under the door to an outlet in the hall. The child was instructed to unplug it as soon as he or she arrived home. So if the alarm went off, we'd wake up to the fact that something had gone wrong. And even if the clock was unplugged before the alarm went off, we had only to look at it in the morning to see what time it had been unplugged. So we always knew *exactly* when the child had arrived home. Sometimes they came excruciatingly close to curfew; rarely were they late. Each one tested us at least once to see whether we were serious about penalizing late arrival. (They found out!)

Now that our kids are adults, we have found that occasionally an alarm still rings. Now, however, it's the "alarm clock" of God's Spirit, alerting us internally as we pray when things aren't right with one of our children. We don't have to stay awake, to leave our place in God's rest, because we know that He is in charge of their lives, and that He will provide wisdom if we will only trust Him.

The Result of Rest

T. S. Eliot has described *rest* as "a lucid stillness that is clear and full of light." Before, we were so busy doing things for our children, so preoccupied with thinking about their problems and ours, we had no leisure for growing. But when we're at rest—when we have ceased from our strivings—we find that there is time to assess, to think, to hear—a time that will bring that clarity which comes with the light of God's wisdom.

It is in that new "time zone" of *rest* that we will find healing. We experience the restoration of frayed nerves, the mending of broken hearts and wounded spirits. We see the Lord at work, creating, caring, loving, giving us strength to go on.

Most wonderfully, He renews in us His peace beyond all understanding. And to reach this place, we must simply trust Him as the only One in the universe who can truly accomplish what must be done in us and in our child.

What habits keep you from entering into a state of rest? See Hebrews 4:9–11.

13

Love Never Fails

What if you try everything you can think of to help your child or to improve your relationship with your child—hope for the best—and the results are long in coming?

What can a troubled parent count on when nothing has made any apparent difference?

Take a cue from the model parent, Mary, the mother of Jesus. Could any human parent experience higher joy than Mary's joy? Could anyone imagine a grief more poignant than her grief? Imagine her delight knowing her newborn Son was the Savior of the world, her happiness as shepherds and wise men came to adore and bring their gifts to Him, her exhilaration as she heard of the angels announcing their "good news of a great joy for all people. Today in the town of David a Savior has been born to you; he is Christ the Lord." She "treasured up all these things and pondered them in her heart."

But there in her heart alongside all the joyful things she pondered, she knew the price that He would have to pay to save His people from their sins; that He would suffer their misery for them and bear the load of their sins on His back.

How did Mary keep going? How did she manage the years of bittersweet pain? The answer is *love.* "Love never fails (or comes to an end)," writes Paul (1 Corinthians 13:8).

The severe love of Mary for her Son continued through suffering, pain, and fear. Who can doubt that, insofar as any human parent could, Mary did everything well? Yet her child met what we would consider a disastrous fate. When there was absolutely nothing more she could do for Him, she loved Him. That love of hers, being the reflected love of God, goes on through eternity.

You, like Mary, have pondered bittersweet thoughts for your child in your heart. Perhaps you have tried everything. You can take Mary's example and love your child with the love of God even if nothing else has produced results. Love never fails. Love is the essence of the character of Jesus, whose Spirit is now in you. As 1 Corinthians 13 explains, "love . . . bears all things, believes all things, hopes all things, endures all things." This amazing love can work its marvels for you when the road seems long and weary.

Love Bears All Things

Let's assume your relationship with your child hasn't improved, even though you've done everything you can think of to make it better. Your child remains in rebellion, or he's pushed away from you emotionally and there is no breaking through his protective barricade. Now what? How do you go on even though you can't see any hope at all in the facts of the situation?

Love: love bears all things. To *bear* something means to move forward while holding it. You don't stand still, in a state of paralysis. On the contrary, you pick up the burden of hard facts and forge ahead. Knowing full well that your child is not right in his relationship to God or to you, you fulfill the law of Christ by carrying his burdens in prayer. You accept him in spite of his sins, not sharing in them, and in this way you are covering a multitude of sins by your love. Far from rejecting your troubled child, you can bear his burden by rolling the heaviness of your heart onto the shoulders of God.

Love Believes All Things

"How gullible can I get, Dr. Backus?" said this distraught father. "I believed every lie Tommy told me. How can I tell lies from truth? The Bible says we're to 'believe all things,' doesn't it? I tried to *believe* him and now look at what's happened. I'm just gullible, I guess. But isn't this how love is supposed to work?"

Do you think this poor man was right? Does love make you a sucker? No way! Jesus didn't automatically buy everything people wanted Him to think. And He taught us to be wise as serpents!

So what does 1 Corinthians mean when it says "love believes all things"? Our interpretation is that it means we ought to be ready to believe the best of our children—unless the facts demonstrate the contrary. We ought not maintain an attitude of cynicism or criticalness. Instead, we believe the best, based on what we see, until facts prove that things are otherwise.

Difficult as it may be—since we have been disappointed so often—we should maintain an optimistic expectation that the situation we've been praying about *will* change for the better one day. This is part of our eager hope in Christ.

This does not mean, however, that we gloss over sin or unrighteousness, compromising the truth. That would be false love. Proverbs 17:15 reminds us: "Acquitting the guilty and condemning the innocent, the Lord detests them both."

Love Hopes and Endures All Things

Many people simply do not believe they can endure the anguish they see ahead of them. We know for certain that it's possible for those who doubt themselves and their fortitude to develop maturity and strength. We've seen them do it. We have witnessed the miraculous growth of courage in some of our clients, friends, and relatives. We think of many who could have become bitter, angry and hopeless. Instead, they have clothed themselves with compassion, kindness, humility, gentleness, and most of all with patience, following the counsel of God (Colossians 3:12–14).

The only way, of course, to hold an unfailing hope for your children is, first, to put your ultimate hope in God. None of us can fall into the weak, even idolatrous position of anchoring our hope in our children. We must ground our peace and security in the One who gives life and freedom, the Lord Jesus Christ.

Those who find this eternal Anchor find growing within them an anticipation—an unexplainable knowledge that their problem child will come, at last, to repentance and restoration. They learn to forego all unrealistic expectations for their children, and at the same time to believe firmly that "with God, nothing is impossible."

These people learn to hang tough, refined by the fires they've come through with their children. They can tell you how it's possible to learn to put up with pain. Finally, one day, you will look back and see how far you've come—and how utterly faithful God has been!

Beyond the Pain

Carl and Kay are known as a "gracious couple." They live out their Christianity, putting others before themselves, serving wherever they're needed in the community or in their church.

The way they have come to be filled with such grace was not easy—but it's a story of remarkable victory.

Years ago, they learned their only child—then, a curly-haired three-year-old daughter—had a rare, slow-growing cancer. For the next thirty years, they all endured ongoing treatments and multiple surgeries. The "gracious couple" has known pain, sorrow, guilt, and fear. They've cried silent tears as they watched their lovely little child deteriorate. Penny has never married.

Despite Penny's *physical* circumstances, Kay can say, "God is sovereign! We will never on this earth see the whole picture. But God sees it, and we trust Him that it is *good*! Our human interpretations are so very limited. What we perceive as bad is sometimes really good, or it can and will be turned to good. Of course, the pain has seemed unbearable at times, but beyond the pain there is hope.

"Our hope is not in ourselves. It's not in doctors, though they've done much to help. Our hope is in God. He has proven himself so faithful these past years to our whole family. It's the Lord who brings us through each day, even when we're sure we can't make it. It was the Lord who strengthened us when Penny got so down she began experimenting with drugs, when she became anoretic, and when she went through treatment and counseling. God was there through it all! What a gift God has given us, making us able to hope in Him!

"Carl and I have made mistakes. Sometimes we've failed the God who's been so faithful to us. But we've done the best we could, and God knows that, just as He knows how frail we are. The future looks bleak for Penny. But we had to decide long ago to go on with our lives. Penny is in the hands of her Creator—safe in His arms. She may at times struggle, or fail, but we can go on with our lives in spite of what she is or does, because God is there to help us all through it. Not only do Carl and I have a responsibility to our child, we also have a responsibility to our community and to our world."

Kay's testimony made us see again that because God's love never fails, even the seemingly impossible situation can be fraught with hope!

The Unfinished Business

Betty came to us one day seeking to resolve a hurt that had possessed her for three years. The police couldn't be sure whether it was an accidental overdose or suicide that had claimed her son's life. All she knew was the torment she and her husband, Scott, endured daily. As she put it, "The torture of the unfinished business."

What haunted her most was the unresolved conflict. The years of David's life had been marked by strife and difficulty. He seemed to be embroiled constantly in troubles of one kind or another. David's death came suddenly, before there was a chance to work out certain issues in their relationship. Had he died knowing how much his parents loved him?

Grief, for these parents, became overwhelming. If only they could have another chance to say all the things that were on their minds.

Gently, we suggested to Betty that it was never too late to express herself, even though David was gone. With that, she decided to write a letter addressed to David. Betty knew she was not "communicating with the dead," yet she had to get her thoughts and feelings out.

Early one morning, she drove out to the cemetery. There, she stood by David's headstone, hearing the sounds of nature around her. She wept as she read aloud what she had written to her only son:

To My Darling David,

I can picture you draped over the chair you always sat in, your long legs dangling, your feet tapping to the music you listened to during most of your waking hours. I can almost reach out and touch the scar over your right eye—you seem so close. How I miss you, David! I'd give anything to have you sitting here, grinning your crooked smile at my attempt to set everything straight.

At night I cry, remembering the days of your childhood. Even through the tears, I laugh at your antics. You could always make me laugh. You could make everyone laugh, no matter how bad things seemed at the time! Somehow you can still magically call forth our laughter.

I have questioned some things I did over the years. Maybe I shouldn't have worked full time when you were a tiny baby. And later, maybe I should have been more involved in your sports and your music. I don't know, but I feel guilty. Did I hurt you? What would you say now if you had the chance?

I need to apologize to you, and ask for your forgiveness for anything I did against you—intentionally or unintentionally. I'm so sorry for the pain I have caused you. Some things are coming to mind even as I write this.

David, I find myself angry with you for leaving us! Why? We could have worked it out. I feel so rejected by you! Did you mean for me to feel this way?

You had so much to give to the world! You are smart, handsome, and witty. See how real you still are to me! I still think of you as alive, here, with us. But you are not! You are gone, forever. And I miss you so much!

I will forever love you, my little boy. I know the Lord loves you even more than your dad and I do. So I give you to Him.

One memory I cherish is the one of you sitting in front of the television watching "Roy Rogers." Your favorite part was the end of the show when Roy and Dale rode along on their horses, Trigger and Buttermilk, singing, "Happy trails to you, until we meet again. . . ." I can almost hear you singing that song to me.

I love you,
Mom

A release of tears, anger and frustration mingled with memories of joy as Betty concluded her letter to her son.

As she drove home, an amazing thing happened. Betty began to rejoice in the gift that was her son's life, and to feel a joyful expectation of their reunion in heaven. From that moment, she focused her hope on the time when she would again see her son, smiling his crooked smile. Even if David couldn't hear her, she had finalized some unfinished business that had eaten at her for three years.

From experiences like Betty's, we've discovered that letter writing can bring healing and restoration, releasing pain that has been held in too long.

Hoping Against Hope

Yes, some situations have a certain finality that may seem to preclude all hope. Yet we believe that it is never "too late" for God, no matter what. Allow the grace of God to envelope you as you turn to Him.

When all is said and done, none of us can predict what God will do with a "hopeless" situation. But we know that, because the God and Father of our Lord Jesus Christ has given us His love, all will be well *in Him*.

Therefore there is hope.

What is your favorite way of showing your child love? In what other ways would he or she enjoy being loved by you? Study 1 Corinthians 13.

14

Joyful Endings

In chapter 4, we introduced you to Karla, who plunged herself into darkness. Yet hers is a story that's turned into a testimony of light, truth and hope.

Today, Karla has completed high school, has moved back to her home and made peace with her parents. In fact, so dramatic is the change in her that the probation officer in charge of Karla's file has thrown away the record, wiping her adolescent slate clean in the eyes of the law.

One day not long ago, this man invited Karla to his home. All over his living room, he'd hung poster-sized pictures of the Karla of former days—punked-out, rebellious, radiating anger. When she walked into the house and saw herself as she'd been, she reeled.

"I had these shots of you blown up big, so you could see the way you *were* contrasted with the *new* Karla. I'm so thrilled with what you've become, Karla, I just had to do something dramatic to tell you." With that, they both burst out laughing with joy.

Currently, Karla is revisiting the old haunts: courtrooms, juvenile lockups, psychiatry wards, and counselors' offices testifying to the change Jesus Christ has wrought in her. She and her parents now discuss life together; she listens respectfully to, and values their advice, and they enjoy

149

one another and their relationship.

If you ask Karla, she'll tell you that her parents did everything *right*, and that she had to go through what she went through to come to the point where God has her.

Few would have predicted such a change. Many would have lost hope. We relate Karla's story for those who cannot now believe their child will ever change—for that's exactly how Roger and Teresa felt about their wayward daughter.

Yet God heard every prayer of their hearts. He heard and answered. Be sure—He will answer yours, too.

Gail: Another Story of Hope

Gail's story will also help to rekindle a flame of expectancy in you. We'll let Gordon, Gail's dad, recount his daughter's odyssey:

"Gail entered her late teens a militant, flaming, neopagan feminist. In her mid-twenties, she began enthusiastically practicing 'good' (or 'white') witchcraft. Gail had been baptized in infancy and nourished in the Christian faith. She'd lived a fervent commitment to her Savior, Jesus Christ. Suddenly, she discarded it all to worship the 'goddess' and venerate the elemental spirits of the universe.

"Our hearts were broken. We grieved for our beloved daughter almost as though she'd died. Over several years, we did everything we could to persuade her to return to the Lord. We worried constantly over the dilemma. If we pushed too hard, we might drive her totally away from us; on the other hand, we couldn't give the impression that her rejecting Christ was a small matter. We tried to strike a balance, never knowing if we were succeeding. Our discussions with her often ended with tears. Gail was respectful and always listened courteously. But she remained rock-like. Our visits together were strained because we no longer shared life's Center. She loved us and we loved her, but the relationship was so painful for all of us we had to strain to maintain it.

"It was especially painful to visit her apartment. To enter her rooms was to be slapped in the face with pictures, artifacts and books proclaiming the tenets of witchcraft.

"We felt our hope dwindling as years went by. What was our testimony to Christ—offered only during our infrequent visits (we lived many hundreds of miles apart)—compared with the power of her total immersion in anti-Christian propaganda? What influence did we have for good? We could see none.

"And all the time, we agonized: What would happen to our beautiful daughter? Spiritually, she was alienated from Jesus Christ. And the radical feminist views she was espousing made the prospects of a healthy marriage unlikely. She had few close friends and was uncomfortable with us and the rest of the family. Despite her excellent education, high intelligence, superb social skills and unusual attractiveness, she found nothing but unhappiness in several attempts to begin a satisfactory career.

"Whenever we saw her struggling, unwilling to turn for help to the Lord, our hearts would sink into near hopelessness. How could anyone or anything help?

"We prayed. Our friends prayed. Every day, for years, we pleaded with God for our daughter. During these years we took comfort from the way God finally drew St. Augustine back to himself after a restless flight into unbelief. Especially, we remembered the unremitting intercession offered by his mother, Monica. Once, she poured out her grief to Bishop Ambrose. Ambrose's response gave her a plank of hope to cling to. 'There is no way,' he assured her, 'that a child of so many tears could be lost.'

"So we prayed, though we saw no results. Then I read an article which suggested that in situations like ours, a person could pray that God would send someone to whom their child *would listen*. We prayed that way—for five long years. Still no sign of change.

"Then, during one of our long-distance phone calls, came the first sign of an answer. 'I hope you're sitting down,' she said, 'because you may faint when you hear what I'm going to say next. I've met a very nice man. You'd like him. He's a Christian!'

"We murmured a prayer of thanksgiving. Did we dare

to believe that this could be the answer to our prayers? Cautiously we stoked our hope. During subsequent phone calls, Gail shared with us the details of their developing relationship and, best of all, of her reawakening interest in the Lord Jesus. The young man, it turned out, was a Pentecostal Christian who, wisely, refused to push his beliefs on Gail. Instead, he made her draw them out of him. It was at her suggestion that he finally took her to his church. She found the simple, joyful worship appealing.

"After that, to our amazement and joy, she bought a Bible. Slowly, she rediscovered the wonderful stories and teachings she'd known and loved as a child. So much was coming back to her, only with a new radiance and a fresh power. We were astonished at what the Lord was doing before our very eyes!

"One night, alone in her apartment, Gail turned on the television set and watched a Billy Graham crusade. She was impressed with Graham's sincerity and clarity. She remembered how, when she'd worked as a TV station employee, she and the others in the studio would hoot their ridicule whenever a religious broadcast was on. This time, she felt no desire to ridicule. She listened. The message, simple and direct, was entitled 'Believe or Die.'

"When the crowds went forward at the end of Billy's message, Gail knelt in the quiet of her apartment and asked the Lord to forgive her—to accept her back as His own! When she got up off her knees she burned her pagan books and symbols. It was the beginning of her pilgrimage back to Christ.

"Not long after, she wrote us a letter, describing her journey back to Jesus Christ. She told of remarkable experiences she'd had during her years as a pagan. Five or six times over the years, she'd heard a voice say clearly in her heart, 'Gail, I love you!' At the time, she'd written it off as a romantic delusion, or thought perhaps it was her 'goddess' speaking. Now she realized it was the Holy Spirit. From time to time, walking along the street, she'd caught herself singing the beautiful words of the *Agnus Dei*, a hymn from the liturgy, which offers the impassioned cry, 'O

Christ, Thou Lamb of God, that takest away the sin of the world, have mercy on us—grant us Thy peace. Amen.' Surprised and angry with herself she'd *will* the song to stop. Later, she'd find herself singing it again in spite of herself!

"These experiences recalled to me a passage of scripture, which can speak very powerfully to travailing parents of older troubled children—especially when that child has wandered from the Lord. James writes of 'the word planted in you, which can save you' (James 1:21). I thought about how we had 'planted' the Word in Gail when she was small—and how through the years of her wandering that 'planted Word' remained inside her, exerting its quiet influence as it was quickened by the Holy Spirit. Now it was growing to fruition. We thought that the Word was lost on her. Now we *know* that God's Word *remains* inside our children, even when they drift from the Lord. It is capable of bearing fruit again, just as it did in our beloved daughter.

"Just when everything seemed to be right again, a new threat appeared on the horizon. Her wonderful new romance fell apart and she was crushed. As she poured out her heart over the telephone, I asked her, 'How is this affecting you spiritually?' We were afraid that her newly restored faith would die with the romance.

" 'When I returned to faith I didn't do it for him,' she answered. 'I thought God sent him to me to be a husband. But He had something even more important in mind—God sent him to bring me back to Jesus.'

"Today, several years later, Gail's journey back to the Lord is complete. She is a mature, radiant, faithful, witnessing Christian. She has married a loving Christian, has a career that's challenging and fulfilling, and she has a stepdaughter whom she is nurturing in the faith!"

To our readers who have prayed for so long and worked so hard to resolve problems with an older child, especially to those who haven't seen any results, we would say only this: Though your own story will differ in detail from Gordon's story of Gail, the core of hope is the same. God has your child in His hand. The implanted Word is still powerful and can, if necessary, break rocks in two. As Bishop Ambrose encouraged Monica, "There is no way that a child of so many tears could be lost."

Your story for your child is not yet finished. Count on God. Let Him restore your hope, your love. Relinquish your child to His hands—and trust Him to write for your family a happy ending to your story.

15

Big Dilemmas

Bob's eighteen-year-old son, Jerry, has been ordered by the court to get in-patient treatment for his drinking problem. Jerry's license has been revoked after his fourth DWI arrest. Jerry doesn't want treatment: He's already completed two previous courses of treatment with no results. He has no money, no job, and no way to get himself out of jail until he enters treatment. Should Bob pay once again for the treatment? Which is worse for Bob? Leaving his son in jail, or wasting his money on what looks like a repeat of previous failures? Which is best for his son?

Twenty-two-year-old Robbie screamed at his parents, "I want you out of my life once and for all! I have no use for you and your stupid Christianity!"

How do they respond to that? Should they "tone down" their Christianity for Robbie's sake? Should they "take a hike" as Robbie demanded? How can they decide what's best for their son? What does the Lord want these parents to do?

Ellie and David's nineteen-year-old daughter will probably die of heart failure if she doesn't recover from the ravages of anorexia. Her 5'9" frame is only skin stretched across bone, for a total weight of 88 pounds. Kate's vital organs are beginning to show signs of degeneration as she continues to starve herself. David and Ellie have been saving money for seven years for the nursing care Ellie will surely need in her struggle with MS. Should they use the money for another hospitalization for their daughter, or should they continue to save for their own dire needs?

None of these problems has an easy solution. Big dilemmas never do. Just when a solution presents itself, another screw is turned, creating further complications.

We have no intention of providing "pat" answers to these dilemmas. Yet it's possible to offer some guidelines to help you prayerfully think your way through the labyrinth.

It will be helpful to define and label your dilemma. When you see it on paper, in front of your eyes, a path toward solution may begin to emerge.

Here is a list of dilemmas we've seen parents of older children trying to work through. Are you facing tough choices like these? Can you add to the list?

- Should I try to force my grown child to go into treatment when he doesn't want it?
- Who pays? Do I? How many times? How important are my own needs by comparison?
- Should I insist on a Christian treatment program?
- Should I let the law deal with my child's illegal behavior or should I try to intervene to protect my child from punishment? Which is best? How do I best help my child?
- Should I call the police and have my own child arrested or should I try to handle him myself even if he seems dangerous?
- Should I speak up on topics I know will offend him if I think they're important and truthful?
- Should I be kind and receptive to his friends even if their behavior often offends my morals and values? Or should I risk driving my child away by offending his friends?

- Should I allow him to bring his lover, male or female, home for a visit? If so, should I forbid them to sleep together under my roof? What if they're upset with my "puritanism"?
- Should I arrange to have my older child deprogramed to get him out of a weird, non-Christian cult? Or should I keep my hands off and just pray?
- Should I let myself love and get attached to my daughter's out-of-wedlock baby? Will I be condoning her lifestyle if I seem to enjoy the little one?
- Should I continue to give him money when he is capable of earning his own but won't hold a job?
- Should I give him money when he uses it frivolously, and keeps wanting more?
- Should I allow my grown child to move home because he wants to save on rent money?
- What can I do if my adult child never gets around to moving to his own quarters even though he is old enough to be on his own?
- Should I provide contraceptives for my seventeen-year-old daughter when she tells me she's sleeping around?
- How do I know when I can trust a child who has often broken trust with me?
- My child is getting a divorce, but my sympathies are with the spouse who is not even my own child. What should I do? What should I say?

Solving a Dilemma—One Step at a Time

Our friends, Ray and Martha, set a courageous example for parents faced with seemingly insoluble conflicts with their adult children.

Their dilemma took shape on the day their twenty-nine-year-old son, Gary, informed them that he and his roommate were homosexual lovers, and that they were planning to be "married." Ray and Martha, reeling from the news, sought advice and help. Could they preserve their own values and standards while maintaining a clear witness to their son and his lover—without sacrificing their relationship with their precious son?

After they'd thought through the issues, investigated the facts, and prayed fervently for guidance, they decided on a policy. They determined to make clear to Gary and his lover their own belief that homosexual behavior is sinful and offensive to God. They resolved that they would not compromise this belief in any way. But they made up their minds to show affection and love to both young men.

To accomplish this, they have made both men welcome in their home and showered them with caring love at Christmastime—but at the outset Ray made it clear to them that, under his roof, they would sleep separately. For Martha in particular, visiting her son's home and staying overnight proved difficult. She set her jaw, though, and forced herself to make such visits. They've made a point never to nag on the subject of sexuality, and at the same time they've continued to make their convictions clear when the issue comes up.

As a result, their relationship with their son has remained close in spite of the obvious moral gap. Martha, to her own amazement, has come to the point of being able to talk with her son on the subject of his sexuality and listen to his feelings, without criticizing—or endorsing—his choice. Even Gary's lover counts Ray and Martha as friends.

Whatever your dilemma, we offer this strategy to help you sort it through.

Think
Investigate
Pray

Think: What is your child's history? Is he bogged down in the mire of selfishness? Is he capable of getting out of the muck? Is he dragging you down with him, or are you able to keep your head above water? Who is getting hurt by your child's behavior? Your child? You? Others? God? What is best for your child? Can you look down the road and see the long-range picture? How does it look to you? Possible or impossible? Why? What does the short-range picture look like? How are your finances? Will your decisions affect them? What can you afford? What do you want to afford? Will it be a waste of your money? What does *your* future look like?

Investigate: What are the *facts* in your child's case? Do you really know the whole story? Can you make the effort to find out? What has your child actually done? Are there others you can talk to, who can add to the facts available to you? Is a life in danger? Is property in danger of being destroyed? Does your child's behavior implicate others? What are the options available for your child? How much will it cost? In money? In emotions? In your relationship to God, to your child? What about the other children in your family—what's happening to them while your energies are expended on your problem child? Are you satisfied with this?

Pray: "Lord, here are my options as far as I can see. All of them look unpleasant. Please show me what I should do. Shine your light on the path of your choosing."

Be alert for an answer to your prayer, which can come in innumerable ways. Be aware that no right answer fits every case. There may be several choices that will be equally right for your situation. The answer to your prayer may come through studying the written Word of God. It may come through circumstances, or it may come as God speaks to you inwardly. Possibly, it will come through a Christian friend or family member.

Remember at all times that the living God is at work in you and in your family. We wait expectantly with you, trusting God to help.

David—who suffered so many tormenting dilemmas in his life—is an encouragement and example for all of us. He asserts, and we can claim with him, by faith:

> "I sought the Lord and he answered me; he delivered me from all my fears. Those who look to him are radiant." (Psalm 34:5)

See 2 Corinthians 4:8. List three dilemmas you are currently experiencing with your child.

16

A Final Word: The Truth About Psychology's "Answers"

Yesterday the father of a young man hospitalized for depression and suicidal impulses came to see us. This man, a good and conscientious person, tried to use the interview to flagellate himself for his son's condition. "I should have done more. I worked so much I didn't spend enough time with him. I should have taken him fishing, hunting, snow-mobiling! I should have played with my family more than I did. My wife says I'm too laid back, too little involved. . . ."

We try to help such self-searching parents, not by showing them where they "went wrong," but by sharing some of what is known about the actual causes of human behavior and helping them understand that they must let other people take responsibility for what they do.

We asked this agitated father, "Did you *never* invite your son to do those things with you?"

"Well, yes," he replied. "I can recall inviting him to go skiing with me not too long ago."

"What happened?"

"He said he didn't feel like going."

Perhaps, as is often the factual truth in such instances, the reluctance to do things together lay more with the son than the father. Yet this father, along with many others, assumed he must be at fault because his son became ill. For many parents today, this is an unfortunate, learned behavior—one that they picked up from Psychology 101!

Ray and Martha were "convinced" by a popular lecturer that they had caused their son to develop homosexual desires—Martha, by being a domineering, over-protective mother; Ray, by distancing himself from his growing son—even though neither one of them fit that mold!

Lynette's twenty-year-old son, Reid, was diagnosed *schizophrenic*. Counselors made her believe Reid's disease was caused by her "schizophrenogenic mothering." She had driven her son into psychosis! Lynette never even questioned whether it was true.

Nancy's adult daughter, Becky, "discovered" during her therapy that Nancy had rejected her when she was a child. Nancy thought she'd tried her best to make her stubborn, cantankerous daughter know she was deeply loved in spite of everything.

Although the best psychologists and psychiatrists have always encouraged their clients to get beyond blaming and parent-bashing, less skillful counselors have unfortunately fostered and encouraged it. Even Christians "ministering" at the altar or in the prayer room have sometimes insisted that in every case the "root" of the problem is mother or father or both. In spite of the fact that psychologists have, for years, questioned and even rejected many of these notions, they have by now percolated through our culture to such an extent that they're commonly accepted. We're not going to argue that parental attitudes and behavior have nothing to do with the future lives of their children. But reasoning *backward* from the existence of a problem, *aiming* at the conclusion that parents must have been at fault, has become too common a practice. The result is that too many good people suffer unfairly.

Psychological Theories

Many parents who blame themselves for their child's problems don't realize that much of what they're telling themselves is out-of-date psychological theory, and not fact at all. Most are unaware that the theories, in fact, change regularly. It's important, therefore, not to crucify yourself or anybody else on the basis of a psychological theory!

Researchers *do not know* all the causes of obsessive-compulsive behaviors, sexual orientation disorders, schizophrenia, manic-depressive psychosis, depressive disorders, or any of the other functional psychiatric disturbances. Even less known are the root causes of most emotional or behavioral problems that torment good parents.

It's also true that even good theories are not absolute truth. Popular speakers and writers do not always mention the important difference between a scientific theory and unchanging truth. A theory is a formulation which, for now, works to explain *some* things investigators observe. It is subject to rejection or alteration, whenever evidence emerges against its validity.[1] And psychological theories about the causes of most disorders—you may be surprised to learn—are rarely founded on adequate experimental data.

We do not want to give the impression that psychologists and psychiatrists are blunderers who don't care whether their theories are supported by data or not. There are several good reasons why theories about behavioral disorders are extremely difficult to support with research.

One reason is that experimenters cannot ethically control human lives precisely enough to isolate the factors they are intending to study. They cannot, for example, take newborn babies and place them with people who will treat them badly in various ways in order to see what effects such treatment will produce later on. It's fine to wallop atoms of hydrogen to smithereens, but it's morally unacceptable to destroy human lives for the sake of scientific progress.

---

[1]Marx, Melvin H., *Theories in Contemporary Psychology* (New York: Macmillan, 1963).

Another difficulty: The experimenter in human psychology is often forced to rely on the recollections of his subjects—not an impressively objective way to obtain unbiased data. Why? People remember selectively. That means that, without being aware of the reasons, we more or less deliberately forget some events and recall others.

Suffice it to say, if you're a parent who is wrung out by guilt feelings, what you learn about the genesis of your child's psychological disturbances is often uncertain. Usually, it's conjectural.

We offer, in fact, one serious concern. Someone has recently reviewed a hundred twenty-five articles published by therapists and counselors, describing children with seventy-two kinds of psychological problems. What is remarkable about the findings is that the mothers of these children were *never* described as psychologically healthy. And *no* mother-child relationship was described as healthy. *Not one.* Is it possible that many counselors operate with a bias against parents which is due, not to ill will, but to training? Could it be that counselors discover fault where so many of their theories have primed them to look?

Let's Look Again at Causes

Are there alternate theories that make sense and do not blame parents?

Yes, there are.

As experimental design in psychiatry and psychology becomes more and more sophisticated, evidence for a *biological component* in behavioral and emotional disorder continues to emerge. (Remember the phrase *biological component.*) This evidence doesn't say that the sole cause of all disorders is physiological, but researchers recognize that biology plays a significant role in a complex network of causal factors.

Take the serious psychological illness schizophrenia, for example. Thirty years ago, the reigning theory about the origin of schizophrenia held that the disease was caused by bad parenting, especially bad mothering. The psychodynamic theorists had even described what they called the *schizophrenogenic mother*. The lady pictured by these theorists was a truly awful person—a woman so bad for her children that she made them gravely ill.

Today, though this theory (incredibly) still has its champions, it would be difficult to find a single expert who does not understand that biological factors play a major part in the onset of schizophrenia. The cumulative weight of the experimental evidence is so great that no one acquainted with it can deny the "basic *biological, physiological, constitutional, and/or genetic* underpinnings of . . . schizophrenia."[2]

A commonly held and frequently cited theory as to the origin of homosexual preference in males—another product of the "blame parents" school—holds that a cold, or aggressive, or rejecting, or distant father plus an overattentive, controlling mother "cause" homosexuality.

Today, an alternative theory about the origin of sexual deviation comes from *behaviorism*. According to this formulation, sexual desire for certain objects is acquired by learning. This theory has not been proven to explain the "cause" of homosexuality, any more than the psychoanalytic theory that fathers and mothers are to blame. But it does offer a reasonable alternative, and illustrates the point: Don't jump to the conclusion that *theory* is the same as final truth, particularly if the theory contradicts your own experience.

Unfortunately, political pressure from the gay rights movement and its supporters has caused both psychiatrists and psychologists to soft-peddle the scientific findings which, to this date, do not furnish any support for the notion that homosexuality is inherited. Most experts who know the research literature on the subject believe that deviant sexual patterns are acquired, probably by the ordinary processes of learning. Each time a developing person experiences sexual arousal and/or orgasm in connection

---

[2]Eron, Leonard D., and Rolf A. Paterson, "Abnormal Behavior, Social Approaches," *Annual Review of Psychology*, Vol. 33, 1982, 31–264, emphasis added.

with an object, the effect is pleasurable reward or reinforcement. Reinforcement following a behavior will raise the probability of its occurring again. Therefore, if a youngster, for whatever reason, fantasizes sexual activity with a person of the same sex while masturbating, and does so repeatedly, the likelihood of developing a homosexual "orientation" becomes high.

Then there are the patients who are suffering from OCD (Obsessive-Compulsive Disorder). These people feel beleaguered by insidious or threatening thoughts that won't go away, or they are compelled to perform senseless, ritualistic, repetitive actions to the point of exhaustion. Sometimes the thoughts and actions go together. Often these patients complain that they must wash their hands dozens of times a day or that they cannot stop checking and rechecking such things as door locks or light switches "just to make sure." All who have studied the thought of Sigmund Freud are familiar with his ingenious theory of the origin of OCD. It was connected, he thought, with overly severe toilet training by a rigid and demanding mother.

Recent research with patients suffering from OCD suggests, however, that obsessions and compulsions are probably *unrelated* to anything whatever in the behavior of parents. Rather, they amount to a kind of mental tic, caused by brain abnormalities—particularly in the biochemistry of one of the most significant neurotransmitting chemicals of the nervous system. Since one of the two effective treatments is a medication and the other a behavior modification procedure, and since psychotherapy based on the old model (or any other psychodynamic model) has no effect on obsessions and compulsions, the new organic theory would seem to have considerable experimental evidence going for it.[3]

Today, as psychological research becomes more cau-

---

[3]An excellent book by a psychiatrist who had been well trained to use the psychodynamic theory before she began specializing in the investigation of Obsessive and Compulsive Disorders is *The Boy Who Wouldn't Stop Washing*, by Judith Rapoport, M.D., published by E.P. Dutton, New York, 1989. This book is a must for a lay person who has been blaming herself or himself for someone else's obsessions or compulsions.

tiously sophisticated, the pitfalls into which we've leaped by rushing to unwarranted conclusions are becoming more apparent.

We could list many more examples of how the theory of parental causation has been weakened by recent psychological research. But the point has been made. Concern for the truth means holding such theories at arms' length—particularly when the Spirit of God has given you the conviction that you are *not* to blame.

Less-Than-Perfect Answers

How does it happen, then, that some children of excellent parents turn out to be rebels, agnostics, social outcasts, neurotics, psychotics, drug abusers, loveless toward their families, sexual deviates, or even criminals and murderers? How?

So far as we know, the perfect experiment to answer all our questions has never been done. But there have been experiments which, though less ambitious and difficult, lead us to question the most commonly accepted theories.

One line of inquiry is a major work over the last few decades by experimenters who wanted to determine how many people are mentally or emotionally disturbed in various cultures. All this work brought an amazing result.

According to common theories, more disorder ought to be found in some places than in others. Certainly, we would expect the quality of parenting to vary in cultures as diverse as those of midtown Manhattan, a Ugandan village, and the country of Iceland. Surely parents don't behave toward their children with absolute uniformity in all those places with such distinctly contrasting folkways. Yet the portion of the population found to have behavioral disorders *does not vary from culture to culture.* Whether we are looking at New Haven or Nigeria, Manhattan or Nova Scotia, Iceland or a Ugandan village, the same figure pops up: 20–25 percent of people exhibit the disorders with which we're concerned. And this figure has not changed over the past thirty-five to forty years!

Either the overall quality of parenting has not varied one bit over time or over cultures, or it has less to do with the development of what is called mental illness than many counselors are willing to admit.

Normal Subjects—Sick Histories

For instance, in one excellent study, experimenters examined a group of patients with the diagnosis of schizophrenia. They carefully matched each patient with a normal person of the same age, sex and general characteristics. Then they studied the histories of both groups, looking for factors usually considered pathogenic—factors like the parental "causes" we've been calling into question.

The results? Twenty-five percent of the *normal* subjects gave histories many counselors would definitely define as traumatic. Yet these persons, who grew up in the midst of such supposedly disturbing conditions, *did not suffer from behavioral disorders or emotional maladjustment.* If this study is representative, it means that one out of every four people has put up with childhood troubles usually considered pathogenic (causing later illness) without becoming disordered.

The experimenters asked questions, looking for the presence or absence of thirty-five unsatisfactory situational factors during childhood. The results were startling. Just as many normal as sick subjects had experienced the same "sickness-causing" conditions. Remember, these are the sorts of conditions parents are regularly blamed for—things that are supposed to make children mentally and emotionally disordered. Does this mean that these commonly accepted "causes of illness" actually have little or nothing to do with later disturbances?

What were some of the supposedly illness-producing conditions for which these histories were examined? They included such unequivocally unhappy factors as poverty, parental alcoholism, divorce and separation, among others.

Remember, the authors of the study did not conclude, nor should we, that these unhappy circumstances have *no* effect on people. The study demonstrates only that, in these subjects at any rate, these factors did not produce behavioral or emotional disorder. Nor were the unhappy circumstances studied the causes of schizophrenia.[4]

Since the completion of that study, other evidence has emerged demonstrating that schizophrenia must be caused in part by inherited physical and/or biochemical abnormalities in the nervous system. Nonetheless, nearly all investigators hold that at least some of the causes of the disease are environmental. This makes the fact that none of the usually accepted "causes" of illness made any difference in the study we've been looking at even more impressive.

"My Parents Were Sick—So I *Must* Need Treatment!"

For several generations, the notion that parents cause mental illness has been so emphatically hammered home that it has become all pervasive. So it sometimes happens that a normal person will seek psychotherapy, believing that because of a troubled home of origin he simply *must* need help.

"But what's wrong? What is it you want help for?" Bill asked one of these would-be clients at the first interview. Test results were normal.

"I need to work on my childhood. My mom left us and ran away with another guy when I was seven."

"So what's your problem *now*?" Bill probed.

"I told you" was the reply. "My dad was left to raise us kids—there were five of us—all by himself. We had some tough times. I thought I ought to get some help."

"Help with *what*? Your psychological tests look good. You don't appear to be depressed or especially nervous. Is anything bothering you about your feelings or your behavior?"

---

[4]Schofield, William, and Balian, Lucy, "A Comparative Study of the Personal Histories of Schizophrenic and Nonpsychiatric Patients." *J abn. soc. psych.*, 1959, *59* (2), 216–225.

"No, I just thought ... Well, I had such a messed-up childhood I thought I should look into it. It could be that something's wrong and I don't know it. Isn't it true that *something's* bound to be wrong with me?"

"Doesn't appear to be," Bill concluded. "I don't think the evidence we have really leads us to the conclusion that you're bound to be sick if you had a troubled home. Some people seem to do fine even with pretty pathological backgrounds. Sounds as if you're one of them."

We finished that session with an agreement that if trouble should turn up later, he could come in and we'd work on it.

This story illustrates how pervasive is the theory that psychopathology and parental mistreatment are virtually two ends of the same stick.

Healthy People: Sick Roots

As a matter of fact, there is evidence that healthy persons often have backgrounds which, according to the theories, *ought* to cause neurosis. Amazingly enough, many successful, emotionally adjusted people were raised by parents who were anything but ideal.

What would you expect to happen if we took the trouble to ask all the questions of normal people that we ask of those who are upset and troubled? You might expect to find the normal people telling of the idyllic families they grew up in. They would tell us how loved they were, how they enjoyed just the right amount of acceptance and just the proper balance of discipline—wouldn't they? They would have spent equal time with mother and father and have loved both equally—don't you suppose? Those paragon parents would have high ratings—wouldn't they?

No. You would be wrong to think that normal people had snug, cozy, conflict-free childhoods.

What *Normal* Folks Recall

Two psychologists, who were not satisfied with the old theories equating bad backgrounds and mental illness, studied a hundred military officers—all normals. These normal people were asked to describe their family backgrounds. With few exceptions they portrayed *conflict* in their families of origin. Not just a little of it—a lot. About 25 percent described not only parental conflicts, but parental rages—open anger and antagonism.

Few of the men recalled their parents as united in the way they disciplined their children. So these normal males felt their training had been less than ideal. Not one thought he had gotten adequate sexual education from his family.

Did they *like* their parents? While two-thirds rated their parents moderately favorable, one-third were disgruntled and dissatisfied with Mom and/or Dad. Few parents seem to have received rave notices.

But when these subjects were rated for adjustment, they were rated "good." Be sure you understand: Well-adjusted people, when interviewed about their parents, said that the people who brought them up were far from ideal![5]

Doctors Serve a Biased Sample

One of the reasons for the present set of theories invoked in psychiatry and psychology is that doctors always work with people who are troubled. We clinicians rarely see normal people. We never gather the histories of those who are *not* asking us for help. We never ask about the parents of high achievers who are doing just fine emotionally. We simply don't know much about those who never darken the door of a psychotherapist.

Very simply—we don't know enough about the incidence of pathogenic factors in the histories of nonpatients, nonclients, nondisturbed, plain ordinary folks. It may very well be that those negative factors from the past, which are assumed to differentiate the disturbed from the nondisturbed, really are not all that different. And if they are not,

[5]Renaud, H. and Estes, F., Life history interviews with one hundred normal American males: "Pathogenicity" of Childhood. *Amer. J. Orthopsychiatry*, 1961, *31*, 786-802.

we have to keep very open minds and look elsewhere for the causes of mental illness.

Our conclusion is this. Too many people take these notions as articles of faith: If anything's wrong with your parents, you have to be sick. And if anything's wrong with you, it has to be the fault of your parents.

Don't you agree that it's time to tell ourselves the truth? Isn't it time to recognize that, just because we don't know why our older problem child has problems, it's not reason enough to conclude that it must be our fault?

In many, many such cases, parents, we must conclude: *It's not your fault!*